About

MW00937005

This booklet is a print version of simplifiedcodes.co....
a more accessible version of the Delaware General Corporation Law
(DGCL), and a Guide to the Federal Proxy Rules. It is current as of
August 1, 2018.

SIMPLIFIED DGCL

The simplified DGCL is a re-write of the DGCL. It rearranges text and
eliminates redundancies. As a result, it is less than half as long as the
original, and hopefully much easier to read. In addition, it facilitates
reading by breaking long paragraphs, inserting paragraph or
subsection titles, and highlighting key terms.

The extent of the re-write differs from section to section, depending on
the opportunities presented by the original statute. Sections 203 and
251 are among the more radically altered sections.

The re-write attempts to "make things as simple as possible, but not
simpler." Its aspiration is to simplify the text without alteration. It even
attempts to preserve ambiguity. Whether this is even possible is of
course controversial.

The proof of the pudding is in the eating. I challenge you to find
mistakes in my simplified version (as judged by the high standard
announced above), and notify me when you do:
hspamann@law.harvard.edu.

The simplified DGCL is complete through section 262. More sections
will follow in the future.

GUIDE TO THE FEDERAL PROXY RULES

The guide to the Federal Proxy Rules takes more liberty with the text
than the simplified DGCL. It is also limited to the more important parts
of the proxy rules, which one is likely to encounter in a law school
course. It comprises rules 14a-1 through 14a-10, skipping 14a-8

(which the SEC has already written in plain language). It merely summarizes or even omits some less important sections (marked by text in square brackets and ellipses, respectively).

ON THE PROPER USE OF THIS BOOKLET

You should use the materials in this booklet only as a learning aid. Ultimately, you must consult the official version of the text. The goal of this booklet is to make that consultation easier, and to demonstrate why it will be worthwhile.

Holger Spamann
August 2018

Contents

Guide to the Federal Proxy Rules 79

Simplified DGCL

Glossary

This simplified version of the Delaware General Corporation Law uses the following shorthand:

- **"board"**: "board of directors of the corporation"
- **"charter"**: "Certificate of Incorporation" (also cf. § 104)
- **"Division of Corporations"**: "Division of Corporations in the Department of State"
- **"qualified foreign corporation"**: "foreign corporation qualified to do business in the State of Delaware" (cf. § 371)
- **"shares"**; **"stock"**: "shares of stock"

Additional shorthand relevant only to an individual section or the subsequent section is defined in those sections. The shorthand is placed in parentheses and quotation marks after the first appearance of the longer, original expression. Sections using additional shorthand include §§ 151, 157, 167/168, 203, 215, 216, 220, 222, 229/230, 245, 251, and 253.

The statute itself defines, inter alia, **"filing"** and **"filing date"** (§ 103), **"principal office"** (§ 131(b)), and **"electronic transmission"** (§ 232(c)).

Any references to statutory provisions without further specification are to sections of this title.

DELAWARE CODE TITLE 8

CORPORATIONS

CHAPTER 1. GENERAL CORPORATION LAW

SUBCHAPTER I. FORMATION

§ 101. Incorporators; how corporation formed; purposes.

(a) Any natural or juridical person may incorporate a corporation under this chapter by filing with the Division of Corporations a charter in accordance with § 103 (a) – (c).

(b) A corporation may be incorporated to conduct or promote any lawful business or purposes.

(c) Corporations for constructing, maintaining and operating public utilities within this State shall also be subject to Title 26.

§ 102. Contents of certificate of incorporation.

(a) **[Mandatory contents]** The charter **shall** set forth:

    (1) **[Name]** The name of the corporation, which shall

        (i) **contain** (or abbreviations thereof, with or without punctuation)

- 1 of the words "association," "company," "corporation," "club," "foundation," "fund," "incorporated," "institute," "society," "union," "syndicate," or "limited," or
- words of like import of foreign countries or jurisdictions (provided they are written in roman characters or letters);

but the Division of Corporations may waive such requirement (unless it determines that such name is, or might otherwise appear to be, that of a natural person)

- if such corporation files in accordance with § 103 (a) – (c) a certificate stating that its total assets, as defined in § 503(i), are not less than $10,000,000, or
- in the Division of Corporations's sole discretion, if the corporation is both a nonprofit nonstock corporation and an association of professionals;

Warning: The legal texts presented here have been altered. Do not rely on them for legal advice

(ii) **distinguish it** on the Division of Corporations's records from any name

- of another domestic corporation,
- of a qualified foreign corporation or any domestic or qualified foreign partnership, LP, LLC, series of an LLC, or statutory trust, or
- that is reserved with the Division of Corporations,

except that in the latter two cases, the Division of Corporations may waive such requirement with the written consent of the name holder or reserver (filed in accordance with § 103 (a) – (c)) or, without prejudice to their rights, in the interest of the state;

(iii) **not contain the word "trust"** (except as permitted by §395); **and**

(iv) **not contain the word "bank"** [unless the corporation is actually a regulated bank etc., or there is no risk of confusion].

(2) **[Registered office]** The address of the corporation's registered office in this State (in accordance with § 131(c)), and the name of its registered agent at such address;

(3) **[Nature of the business]** The nature of the business or purposes to be conducted or promoted. It shall be sufficient to state, either alone or with other businesses or purposes, that the purpose of the corporation is to engage in any lawful act or activity for which corporations may be organized under this chapter;

(4) **[Share classes and rights]** The total number of shares of all classes of stock authorized to be issued; and for each class of shares the number of shares and their par value (or a statement that the class is to be without par value); and, if and in as far as desired, in respect of any class or series of stock, a statement of, or an express grant of authority to the board to fix by resolution, the designations, powers, rights, and qualifications thereof, which are permitted by § 151;

OR, in the case of a **nonstock** corporation, the fact that the corporation is a nonstock corporation. A nonstock corporation shall have members but it is not dissolved, and its acts are still valid, even if it does not have members. A nonstock corporation's charter or bylaws

---

- shall set forth the criteria for identifying members (otherwise, those entitled to elect the governing body shall be deemed members);
- may establish, or make provision to establish in the future, different member groups or classes with differential rights or duties.

(5) **[Incorporators]** The name and mailing address of the incorporators;

(6) **[First directors]** If the powers of the incorporators are to terminate upon the filing of the charter, the names and mailing addresses of the persons who are to serve as directors until the first annual meeting of stockholders or until their successors are elected and qualify.

(b) **[Optional contents]** The charter (may) also contain:

(1) **[General Enabling Clause]** "**Any provision** for the management of the business and for the conduct of the affairs of the corporation, and any provision creating, defining, limiting and regulating the powers of the corporation, the directors, and the stockholders, or any class of the stockholders, or the governing body, members, or any class or group of members of a nonstock corporation; if such provisions are **not contrary to the laws of this State.** Any provision which is required or permitted by any section of this chapter to be stated in the bylaws may instead be stated in the certificate of incorporation;"

(2) **[court-approved compromise]** [a clause set forth in the statute, to be reproduced verbatim, allowing for a compromise approved by ¾ in value of each class of creditors and stockholders/members and sanctioned by a Delaware court of equity, which will be binding on all creditors and stockholders of that class];

(3) **[preemptive rights]** Provisions granting to the holders of stock of the corporation, or of any class or series thereof, the preemptive right to subscribe to any or all additional issues of any or all classes or series of stock of the corporation, or to any securities of the corporation convertible into such stock. [No preemptive rights unless explicitly set forth in charter; grandfathering clause for rights in existence on July 3, 1967];

(4) **[supermajority provisions]** Provisions requiring for any corporate action the vote of a larger portion than is required by this chapter;

(5) **[duration]** "A provision limiting the duration of the corporation's existence to a specified date; otherwise, the corporation shall have perpetual existence;"

(6) **[personal liability]** "A provision imposing personal liability for the debts of the corporation on its stockholders to a specified extent and upon specified conditions; otherwise, the stockholders ... shall not be personally liable for the payment of the corporation's debts except as they may be liable by reason of their own conduct or acts;"

(7) **[limit on director liability]** "A provision **eliminating or limiting** the personal liability of a director to the corporation or its stockholders for **monetary damages** for breach of fiduciary duty as a director," *except:*

   (i) For breaches of the **duty of loyalty**;

   (ii) "for acts or omissions **not in good faith** or which involve **intentional misconduct** or a **knowing violation of law**;"

   (iii) under § 174; or *unlawful payment dividends; effectively null since directors set capital* "⇒ §154

   (iv) "for any transaction from which the director derived an **improper personal benefit**."

No such provision can limit liability incurred prior to the date when such provision becomes effective. The term 'director' in this paragraph includes all other persons who, pursuant to a provision of the charter in accordance with § 141(a), exercise or perform board powers or duties.

(c) **[Unnecessary contents]** "It shall not be necessary to set forth in the certificate of incorporation any of the powers conferred on corporations ✓ by this chapter."

(d) **[Reference to facts outside the charter]** Except for provisions included pursuant to (a)(1), (a)(2), (a)(5), (a)(6), (b)(2), (b)(5), (b)(7), and provisions included pursuant to (a)(4) specifying the classes, number of shares, and par value of authorized shares, any provision of the charter may be made dependent upon facts ascertainable outside such instrument, provided that the manner in which such facts shall operate upon the provision is clearly and explicitly set forth therein. The term "facts," as used in this subsection, includes the occurrence of any event, including a determination or action by any person or body, including the corporation.

(e) **[Reserving a name]** A name can be reserved for 120 days by or on behalf of anyone contemplating to use that name for a domestic or qualified foreign corporation. The reservation is renewable and transferable. Reservation, renewal, transfer, or cancellation are made by filing with the Secretary of State including the reserved name, the name and address of the applicant or transferee, and a filing fee as specified in § 391. If the filing is in conformity with law, the Secretary of State shall return to the applicant a copy of the filing with a notice of the action taken.

(f) **[No fee-shifting]** "The certificate of incorporation may not contain any provision that would impose liability on a stockholder for the attorneys' fees or expenses of the corporation or any other party in connection with an internal corporate claim, as defined in § 115 of this title."

would discourage derivative suits; impact governance

§ 103. Execution, acknowledgment, filing, recording and effective date of original certificate of incorporation and other instruments; exceptions.

(a) **[Execution]** Any **instrument to be filed** in accordance with this chapter shall be executed as follows:

(1) The **charter**, and any other instrument to be filed before the election or nomination of the initial board, shall be signed by the incorporator(s). If any incorporator is not available, then any such other instrument may be signed by any person for whom such incorporator, in executing the charter, was acting, provided that such other instrument shall state these circumstances.

(2) "All **other instruments** shall be signed:

    a. By any authorized officer of the corporation; or

    b. If it shall appear from the instrument that there are no such officers, then by a majority of the directors or by such directors as may be designated by the board; or

    c. If it shall appear from the instrument that there are no such officers or directors, then by the holders of record, or such of them as may be designated by the holders of record, of a majority of all outstanding shares of stock; or

    d. By the holders of record of all outstanding shares of stock."

(b) **[Acknowledgment]** Any instrument to be acknowledged under this chapter must contain either:

    (1) The formal acknowledgment by a person signing the instrument that it is the act/deed of such person or of the corporation, and that the facts stated therein are true. Such acknowledgment shall be made before a person who is authorized by the law of the place of execution to take acknowledgments of deeds. If such person has a seal of office such person shall affix it to the instrument.

    (2) The signature, without more, of the person(s) signing the instrument, in which case such signature(s) shall constitute the affirmation or acknowledgment of the signatory, under penalties of perjury, that the instrument is the act/deed of such person or of the corporation, and that the facts stated therein are true.

(c) **[Filing] Filing requirements** in this chapter mean that:

    (1) The signed instrument shall be delivered to the office of the Secretary of State;

    (2) All ancillary taxes and fees shall be tendered to the Secretary of State; and

    (3) The Secretary of State records the date and time of delivery, and, when the required taxes and fees are also tendered, certifies filing by endorsing upon the signed instrument the word "Filed", and the date and time of its filing. This endorsement is the "filing date", and is conclusive of the date and time of filing in the absence of actual fraud. …

    (4) The filing date may be post-dated upon request made on or prior to delivery. If the Secretary of State refuses filing due to an imperfection, it may hold such instrument in suspension and, if a replacement instrument is properly filed within 5 business days after notice of such suspension is given to the filer, establish as the filing date the date and time of delivery of the rejected instrument. …

    (5) – (7) [Division of filing fees between Secretary of State, counties, and municipalities]

---

(8) Appropriate information from filed instruments is to be entered into the Delaware Corporation Information System and to be permanently maintained as a public record on a suitable medium. ...

(d) **[Effectiveness of filed instruments]** Any instrument filed in accordance with subsection (c) shall be effective upon its filing date, unless it provides a later effective date (maximum 90 days after the filing date; prior to such later date, such instrument may be terminated, or its effective date be amended, by the filing of a certificate of termination or amendment).

(e) **[Special provisions]** Subsections (a) to (d) do not apply to the extent other sections contain differing specific rules.

(f) **[Corrections]** Filed instruments may be corrected by filing a certificate of correction or a corrected instrument (entitled as such), explaining the inaccuracy, if the original instrument is an inaccurate record of the corporate action or was defectively or erroneously executed, sealed or acknowledged. The corrected instrument shall be effective as of the date the original instrument was filed, except as to those persons who are substantially and adversely affected by the correction.

(g) **[No liability of Secretary of State]** The Secretary of State shall have no liability for the filing or indexing of defective instruments.

(h) **[Facsimile and electronic signatures]** Any required signature may be a facsimile, a conformed signature or an electronically transmitted signature.

(i) **[Pre-dating of filing in extraordinary conditions]** [If an instrument could not be filed on a certain date due to 'extraordinary conditions', the Secretary of State may nevertheless establish such date as the filing date if the instrument is filed within a reasonable period (maximum 2 days) after the cessation of such 'extraordinary conditions'. 'Extraordinary conditions' are defined to include emergency resulting from war, natural disaster, rioting, etc., or closing down of the Secretary of State's office because of telephone or electricity outage etc.]

(j) [No separate filing required to comply with § 131(c)] ...

---

§ 104. Certificate of incorporation; definition.

The term "certificate of incorporation," unless the context requires otherwise, includes not only the original charter filed to create a corporation but also all other instruments, howsoever designated, which are filed pursuant to any section of this title, and which have the effect of amending or supplementing a corporation's original charter.

§ 105. Certificate of incorporation and other certificates; evidence.

A copy of a charter shall, when duly certified by the Secretary of State, be received in all courts, public offices and official bodies as prima facie evidence of:

(1) Due execution, acknowledgment and filing of the instrument;

(2) Observance and performance of all acts and conditions necessary to have been observed and performed precedent to the instrument becoming effective; and

(3) Any other facts required or permitted by law to be stated in the instrument.

§ 106. Commencement of corporate existence.

From the date of the filing with the Secretary of State of the charter in accordance with § 103, the incorporator(s) who signed the certificate constitute a body corporate, by the name set forth in the certificate, subject to subsection § 103(d) and subject to dissolution or other termination of its existence as provided in this chapter.

§ 107. Powers of incorporators.

Until the nomination or election of the first directors, the incorporator(s) shall manage the affairs of the corporation and may do whatever is necessary and proper to perfect the organization of the corporation, including the adoption of the original bylaws and the election of directors.

§ 108. Organization meeting of incorporators or directors named in charter.

(a) After the filing of the charter, an organization meeting of the incorporator(s), or of the board if the initial directors were named in the charter, shall be held, at the call of a majority of the incorporators/directors, for the purposes of adopting bylaws, electing directors (if the meeting is of the incorporators) to serve until the first

---

Warning: The legal texts presented here have been altered. Do not rely on them for legal advice

annual meeting of stockholders, electing officers (if the meeting is of the directors), doing any other acts to perfect the organization of the corporation, and transacting any other business.

(b) The persons calling the meeting shall give at least 2 days' written notice thereof by any usual means of communication, including the meeting's time, place and purposes. Notice need not be given to anyone who attends the meeting or who signs a waiver of notice either before or after the meeting.

(c) Any action permitted to be taken at the organization meeting may be taken without a meeting if each incorporator or director signs an instrument which states the action so taken.

(d) If any incorporator is not available to act under this section or § 107, then any person for whom the incorporator was acting directly or indirectly as employee or agent, may take such action; provided that the instrument or minutes, as the case may be, state the aforegoing and the reason for the incorporator's inability, and that such person's signature or participation is otherwise authorized and not wrongful.

§ 109. Bylaws.

(a) **The power to adopt,** amend, or repeal bylaws of a stock/nonstock corporation shall always be in the stockholders/members entitled to vote; provided, however, that the charter may confer such power *also* (i.e., not exclusively) upon the directors/governing body. The incorporators and initial directors/governing body named in the charter may adopt, amend, or repeal the bylaws; the board of a stock corporation may do so only before the corporation has received any payment for any of its stock.

(b) "The **bylaws may contain** *any* **provision,** [not inconsistent with law or with the charter] relating to the business of the corporation, the conduct of its affairs, and its rights or powers or the rights or powers of its stockholders, directors, officers or employees. The bylaws **may *not* contain** any provision that would impose liability on a stockholder for the attorneys' fees or expenses of the corporation or any other party in connection with an internal corporate claim, as defined in § 115 of this title."

§ 110. Emergency bylaws and other powers in emergency.

[During catastrophes such as attacks, nuclear disaster etc., emergency bylaws inconsistent with law and the charter may be adopted, rules for convening of meetings may be disregarded, officer and director liability is limited to wilful misconduct, etc.]

§ 111. Jurisdiction to interpret, apply, enforce or determine the validity of corporate instruments and provisions of this title.

The Court of Chancery has jurisdiction over any civil action to interpret, apply, enforce, or, in the case of (a), determine the validity of

(a)

(1) the charter and bylaws,

(2)(i)/(ii)   any instrument by which a corporation (i) creates or sells, or offers to create or sell, any of its stock or any rights respecting its stock; or (iii), if conditioned on approval by one or more stockholders, agrees to sell, lease or exchange any of its property or assets,

(2)(iii) any instrument to which the corporation is a party and pursuant to which a stockholder sells or offers to sell any of its stock,

(3) any restriction on transfer or ownership under § 202,

(4) any proxy under § 212 or 215,

(5) any voting trust or agreement under § 218,

(6)-(9) any instrument required by any provision of this title,

except to the extent that a statute confers exclusive jurisdiction on another court, agency or tribunal; or

(b)   any provision of this title.

§ 112. Access to proxy solicitation materials.

The bylaws may provide that if the corporation solicits proxies with respect to an election of directors, it must include in its proxy solicitation materials individuals nominated by a stockholder. The requirement may be subject to any lawful procedures or conditions, such as ...

... requiring from the nominating stockholder:

Warning: The legal texts presented here have been altered. Do not rely on them for legal advice

(1) minimum stock ownership, including duration; this can take into account options or other rights relating to the stock;

(2) submission of specified information concerning the stockholder and its nominees, including information concerning ownership of the corporation's stock or options;

(5) an undertaking to indemnify the corporation in respect of any loss arising as a result of any false or misleading information or statement submitted in connection with a nomination;

... excluding nominations by:

(4) any person who has directly or indirectly acquired or publicly proposed to acquire shares constituting a specified percentage of the voting power within a specified period before the election of directors; and

... conditioning eligibility on:

(3) the number or proportion of directors nominated by stockholders, and whether the stockholder previously sought such inclusion.

§ 113. Proxy expense reimbursement.

"(a) <u>The bylaws may provide for the reimbursement by the corporation of expenses incurred by a stockholder in soliciting proxies in connection with an election of directors, subject to such procedures or conditions as the bylaws may prescribe</u>, including:

(1) Conditioning eligibility for reimbursement upon the number or proportion of persons nominated by the stockholder seeking reimbursement or whether such stockholder previously sought reimbursement for similar expenses;

(2) Limitations on the amount of reimbursement based upon the proportion of votes cast in favor of 1 or more of the persons nominated by the stockholder seeking reimbursement, or upon the amount spent by the corporation in soliciting proxies in connection with the election;

(3) Limitations concerning elections of directors by cumulative voting pursuant to § 214 of this title; or

(4) Any other lawful condition.

(b) No bylaw so adopted shall apply to elections for which any record date precedes its adoption."

§ 114. Application of chapter to nonstock corporations.

(a) Except as specified in subsections (b) and (c), the provisions of this chapter and chapter 5 of this title [i.e, the provisions regarding the corporation franchise tax] apply to nonstock corporations in the following manner:

   (1) All references to stockholders refer to members of the corporation;

   (2) All references to the board refer to the governing body of the corporation;

   (3) All references to directors or to members of the board refer to members of the governing body; and

   (4) All references to stock, capital stock, or shares thereof refer to memberships of a nonprofit nonstock corporation and to membership interests of any other non-stock corporation.

(b) Subsection (a) shall not apply to:

   (1) "Sections 102(a)(4), (b)(1) and (2), 109(a), 114, 141, 154, 215, 228, 230(b), 241, 242, 253-258, 271, 276, 311-313, 390, and 503 of this title, which apply to nonstock corporations by their terms;"

   (2) "Sections 102(f), 109(b) (last sentence), 151-153, 155, 156, 157(d), 158, 161-168, 205, 211-214, 216, 219, 222, 231, 243, 244, 251, 252, 267, 274, 275, 324, 391, and 502(a)(5) of this title; and"

   (3) "Subchapter XIV [close corporations] and subchapter XV [public benefit corporations] of this chapter."

(c) In the case of a nonprofit nonstock corporation, subsection (a) shall not apply to:

   (1) The sections and subchapters listed in subsection (b);

   (2) Sections 102(b)(3), 111(a)(2) and (3), 144(a)(2), 217, 218(a) and (b), and 262; and

   (3) Subchapter V [stocks and dividends] and subchapter VI [stock transfers] (other than sections 204 and 205).

(d) For purposes of this chapter:

(1) "A "charitable nonstock corporation" is any nonprofit nonstock corporation that is exempt from taxation under § 501(c)(3) of the United States Internal Revenue Code, or any successor provisions."

(2) A "membership interest" is, unless otherwise provided in the charter, a member's share of the profits and losses of a nonstock corporation, or a member's right to receive distributions of the nonstock corporation's assets, or both;

(3) "A "nonprofit nonstock corporation" is a nonstock corporation that does not have membership interests; and"

(4) "A "nonstock corporation" is any corporation organized under this chapter that is not authorized to issue capital stock."

§ 115. Forum selection provisions.

Internal affairs Doctrine

The charter or bylaws may require, and <u>cannot prohibit, that internal corporate</u> <u>claims be brought (only) in Delaware.</u> "'Internal corporate claims' means claims, including claims in the right of the corporation, (i) that are based upon a violation of a duty by a current or former director or officer or stockholder in such capacity, or (ii) as to which this title confers jurisdiction upon the Court of Chancery."

SUBCHAPTER II. POWERS

§ 121. General powers.

(a) In addition to the powers enumerated in § 122, a corporation has all the powers granted by this chapter or by any other law or by its certificate of incorporation, together with any powers incidental thereto, so far as such powers and privileges are necessary or convenient to the conduct, promotion or attainment of the business or purposes set forth in its certificate of incorporation.

(b) Every corporation shall be governed by the provisions and be subject to the restrictions and liabilities contained in this chapter.

§ 122. Specific powers.

Corporations have **power** to:

(1) Have perpetual succession by its corporate name, unless a limited period of duration is stated in its certificate of incorporation;

(2) Sue and be sued in all courts and participate, as a party or otherwise, in any judicial, administrative, arbitrative or other proceeding, in its corporate name;

(3) Have, use, and change a corporate seal;

(4) Own, deal in or with, any property, or any interest therein;

(5) "Appoint such officers and agents as the business of the corporation requires and to pay or otherwise provide for them suitable compensation;"

(6) "Adopt, amend and repeal bylaws;"

(7) "Wind up and dissolve itself in the manner provided in this chapter;"

(8) "**Conduct its business**, carry on its operations and have offices and exercise its powers **within or without this State**;"

(9) "**Make donations** for the public welfare or for charitable, scientific or educational purposes, and in time of war or other national emergency in aid thereof;"

(10) "Be an incorporator, promoter or manager of other corporations of any type or kind;"

(11) Participate with others in any association of any kind, or in any arrangement which the participating corporation would have power to conduct by itself, whether or not such participation involves sharing or delegation of control with or to others;

(12) Transact any lawful business which the corporation's board of directors shall find to be in aid of governmental authority;

(13) Make all kinds of contracts, including finance contracts, and make contracts of guaranty and suretyship which are necessary or convenient to the conduct, promotion or attainment of the business of single-shareholder parent or grand-parent or wholly-owned subsidiary corporations, "which contracts of guaranty and suretyship shall be deemed to be necessary or convenient to the conduct, promotion or attainment of the business of the contracting corporation, and make other contracts of guaranty and suretyship which are necessary or convenient

to the conduct, promotion or attainment of the business of the contracting corporation;"

(14) Lend, invest and reinvest funds, and take security for such funds;

(15) Pay pensions and establish and carry out pension and compensation plans, for any or all of its directors, officers and employees, or those of its subsidiaries;

(16) Provide insurance for its benefit on the life of any of its directors, officers or employees, or on the life of any stockholder for the purpose of acquiring at such stockholder's death shares of its stock owned by such stockholder.

(17) Renounce, in its certificate of incorporation or by action of its board of directors, any interest or expectancy of the corporation in specified business opportunities or specified classes or categories of business opportunities that are presented to the corporation or 1 or more of its officers, directors or stockholders.

§ 123. Powers respecting securities of other corporations or entities.

Corporations may own, deal in and with, and exercise all rights of, all types of securities.

§ 124. Effect of lack of corporate capacity or power; ultra vires.

Acts of a corporation (including transfer of property) shall not be invalid by reason of the lack of capacity or power of the corporation to do such act, but such lack of capacity or power may be asserted:

(1) In a proceeding **by a stockholder against the corporation to enjoin a corporate act**. If such unauthorized acts are being performed pursuant to any contract to which the corporation is a party, the court may, if all of the parties to the contract are parties to the proceeding and if it deems the same to be equitable, set aside and enjoin the performance of such contract, and in so doing may allow to the corporation or to the other parties to the contract, as the case may be, equitable compensation for their loss from the court's setting aside and enjoining the performance of such contract, but anticipated profits to be derived from the performance of the contract shall not be awarded by the court as a loss;

(2) In a proceeding **by the corporation against its incumbent or former officer or director, for loss** or damage due to such officer's or director's unauthorized act;

(3) In a proceeding **by the Attorney General to dissolve the corporation, or to enjoin** the corporation from the transaction of unauthorized business.

§ 125. Conferring academic or honorary degrees.

[power to confer academic degree dependent on permission by Department of Education]

§ 126. Banking power denied.

(a) The corporation does not have the power to issue evidences of debt for circulation as money, or the power of carrying on the business of receiving deposits of money.

(b) Corporations organized to buy, sell and otherwise deal in notes, open accounts and other similar evidences of debt, or to loan money and to take notes, open accounts and other similar evidences of debt as collateral security therefor, shall not be deemed to be engaging in the business of banking.

§ 127. Private foundation; powers and duties.

"A corporation of this State which is a private foundation under the US internal revenue laws and whose charter does not expressly provide that this section shall not apply to it is required to act or to refrain from acting so as not to subject itself to the taxes imposed by 26 U.S.C. § 4941 (relating to taxes on self-dealing), 4942 (relating to taxes on failure to distribute income), 4943 (relating to taxes on excess business holdings), 4944 (relating to taxes on investments which jeopardize charitable purpose), or 4945 (relating to taxable expenditures), or corresponding provisions of any subsequent US internal revenue law."

SUBCHAPTER III. REGISTERED OFFICE AND REGISTERED AGENT

§ 131. Registered office in State; principal office or place of business in State.

(a) Every corporation shall maintain in this State a registered office, which need not be the same as its place of business.

Warning: The legal texts presented here have been altered. Do not rely on them for legal advice

(b) In any document or statute, unless the context requires otherwise, the term "corporation's principal office or place of business in this State" or "principal office or place of business of the corporation in this State," or other term of like import, shall be deemed to mean the corporation's registered office.

(c) In any document filed with the Secretary of State under this chapter, the address of a registered office shall include the street, number, city, country, and postal code.

§ 132. Registered agent in State; resident agent.

(a) Every corporation shall maintain in this State a registered agent, which can be

    (1) the corporation itself;

    (2) an individual resident of Delaware;

    (3) a domestic "entity" (corporation, general or limited partnership, LLC, or statutory trust); or

    (4) a foreign entity.

(b) Every registered agent shall

    (1)

- if an entity, maintain a business office in Delaware which is generally open, or
- if an individual, be generally present at a designated location in Delaware,
- at sufficiently frequent times to perform the functions of a registered agent, in particular to accept service of process;

    (2) if a foreign entity, be authorized to transact business in Delaware;

    (3) accept and forward service of process and other communications to its corporations;

    (4) forward to its corporations the annual franchise tax report required by §502 or an electronic notification of same in a form satisfactory to the Secretary of State.

(c) Any registered agent who at any time serves as registered agent for more than 50 entities (a "commercial registered agent") shall satisfy and comply with the following qualifications: ...

(d) Every corporation shall provide to its registered agent, and the registered agent shall retain, the name, business address, and business telephone number of a natural person who is then deemed the communications contact and authorized to receive communications from the registered agent. The corporation shall update this information as necessary. If the corporation fails to provide a current communications contact, the registered agent may resign pursuant to §136.

(e) The Secretary is authorized to issue such rules and regulations as may be necessary or appropriate to carry out the enforcement of subsections (b), (c) and (d), and to take actions reasonable and necessary to assure registered agents' compliance with these subsections. Such actions may include refusal to file documents submitted by a registered agent.

(f) Upon application of the Secretary, the Court of Chancery may enjoin any person or entity from serving as a registered agent or as an officer, director or managing agent of a registered agent. ...

(g) The Secretary is authorized to make a list of registered agents available to the public, and to establish such qualifications and issue such rules and regulations with respect to such listing as the Secretary deems necessary or appropriate.

(h) In any document or statute, unless the context requires otherwise, the term "resident agent" or "resident agent in charge of a corporation's principal office or place of business in this State," or other term of like import, shall be deemed to mean, the corporation's registered agent.

§ 133. Change of location of registered office; change of registered agent.

A corporation may, by resolution of its board, change the location of its registered office, and/or its registered agent, within this State. The resolution shall contain the information required by § 102(a)(2), and be filed in accordance with § 103 (a) – (c).

§ 134. Change of address or name of registered agent.

By filing a certificate in accordance with § 103 (a) – (c), a registered agent may change

(a) the address of the registered office of the corporation(s) for which the agent is a registered agent to another address in this State; or

(b) its name.

§ 135. Resignation of registered agent coupled with appointment of successor.

The registered agent may resign and appoint a successor by filing a certificate to this effect in accordance with § 102(a)(2) and § 103 (a) – (c). There shall be attached to such certificate a statement of each affected corporation approving such change, executed and acknowledged in accordance with § 103. …

§ 136. Resignation of registered agent not coupled with appointment of successor.

(a) The registered agent may resign without appointing a successor by acknowledging and filing a certificate of resignation, but such resignation shall not become effective until 30 days after the certificate is filed. The certificate shall contain a statement that written notice of resignation was given to each affected corporation at least 30 days prior to the filing by mailing or delivering such notice to the corporation at its address last known to the registered agent and shall set forth the date of such notice.

(b) After receipt of the aforesaid notice of resignation, the corporation shall designate a new registered agent as provided in § 133. If the corporation fails to do so before the resignation of the registered agent becomes effective, the Secretary of State shall forfeit, in case of a domestic corporation, its charter, and in case of a foreign corporation, its authority to do business in this State, …

(c) … and service of legal process against the corporation shall thereafter be upon the Secretary of State in accordance with § 321.

SUBCHAPTER IV. DIRECTORS AND OFFICERS

§ 141. Board of directors; powers; number, qualifications, terms and quorum; committees; classes of directors; nonstock corporations; reliance upon books; action without meeting; removal.

(a) [General management powers] "The business and affairs of every corporation organized under this chapter shall be managed by or under the direction of a board of directors, except as may be otherwise provided

---

in this chapter or in its charter. If any such provision is made in the charter, the powers and duties conferred or imposed upon the board of directors by this chapter shall be exercised or performed to such extent and by such person or persons as shall be provided in the charter."

(b) **[Composition of the board]** The board shall consist of 1 or more natural persons. The charter or bylaws may prescribe other qualifications for directors (e.g., to be a stockholder). Their number shall be fixed by, or in the manner provided in, the charter or the bylaws.

[Term] Each director holds office until his/her replacement, removal or resignation. Any director may resign at any time upon notice given in writing or by electronic transmission to the corporation. The resignation is effective upon delivery unless it specifies a later date or a condition. A resignation conditioned upon the director failing to receive a specified vote for reelection may provide that it is irrevocable.

[Quorum] A majority of the total number of directors shall constitute a quorum. The charter or the bylaws may require a greater or lesser number (no less than 1/3).

[Majority decision] "The vote of the majority of the directors present at a meeting at which a quorum is present shall be the act of the board unless the charter or the bylaws shall require a vote of a greater number."

(c) **[Committees]** (Paragraph (1) applies to any corporation incorporated prior to July 1, 1996, unless it decides by a majority resolution of the whole board to be governed by paragraph (2). Paragraph (2) applies to any corporation incorporated on or after July 1, 1996.)

(1) [Same as paragraph (2), except that (a) the board resolution instating the committee must in all cases be passed by a majority of the whole board, and (b) the delegable powers are enumerated individually in paragraph (1) (but the substance seems to be the same)]

(2) The board may designate **committees** of 1 or more directors. Any such committee, to the extent provided in the resolution of the board, or in the bylaws, exercises **all the powers of the board, except**: (i) approving or adopting, or recommending to the stockholders, any matter (other than the election or removal of directors) expressly

---

required by this chapter to be submitted to stockholders for approval or (ii) adopting, amending or repealing bylaws.

The board may designate directors as alternate members of any committee, who may replace any absent or disqualified member at any committee meeting. The bylaws may provide that in the absence or disqualification of a committee member at a meeting, the other member(s), whether or not such member(s) constitute a quorum, may unanimously appoint another director as replacement member for such meeting.

(3) Unless otherwise provided in the charter, the bylaws or the resolution of the board designating the committee, a committee may create **subcommittees** of 1 or more committee members, and delegate to a subcommittee any or all of the committee's powers. Except in this subsection (c), every reference in this chapter to a committee includes a subcommittee.

(4) Quorum and majority requirements for committees are determined by the same rules as for the full board, except that permitted deviations from the default can also be contained in a resolution of the board, or of the committee that created the subcommittee.

(d) **[Staggered board]** The charter, an *initial* bylaw, or a bylaw *adopted by a stockholder vote*, may divide the directors into up to 3 classes, whose terms of office expire in successive years beginning with class 1 at the first annual meeting after the classification becomes effective. This charter or bylaw provision, as the case may be, may authorize the board then in office to assign its members to the newly created classes.

[Classified board] The charter may confer upon holders of any class or series of stock the right to elect 1 or more directors with such term and voting powers as stated in the charter, which may be greater or less than those of other directors.

[Differential voting rights] More generally, the charter may confer upon any 1 or more directors voting powers greater than or less than those of other directors, including in committee votes. In any such case of unequal director voting rights, every reference in this chapter to a majority or other

Warning: The legal texts presented here have been altered. Do not rely on them for legal advice

22

proportion of the directors shall refer to a majority or other proportion of the votes of the directors.

(e) **[Reliance on documents and reports]** A member of the board or any committee shall, "in the performance of such member's duties, be **fully protected in relying in good faith upon** the records of the corporation and upon such information, opinions, reports or statements presented to the corporation by any of the corporation's **officers or employees**, or **committees** of the board of directors, **or** by any other person as to matters the member reasonably believes are within such other person's **professional or expert competence** and who has been **selected with reasonable care** by or on behalf of the corporation."

(f) **[Action without a meeting]** Unless otherwise restricted by the charter or bylaws, the board or any committee may take any action without a meeting if all members consent thereto in writing or by electronic transmission, and the writing(s) or electronic transmission(s) are filed with the minutes (in paper or electronic form, depending on how such minutes are kept).

[Advance consent] "Any person (whether or not then a director) may provide, whether through instruction to an agent or otherwise, that a consent to action will be effective at a future time (including a time determined upon the happening of an event), no later than 60 days after such instruction is given or such provision is made and such consent shall be deemed to have been given for purposes of this subsection at such effective time so long as such person is then a director and did not revoke the consent prior to such time. Any such consent shall be revocable prior to its becoming effective."

(g) **[Place of meetings]** Unless otherwise restricted by the charter or bylaws, the board may hold its meetings, and have offices, outside of this State.

(h) **[Authority to set director remuneration]** Unless otherwise restricted by the charter or bylaws, the board shall have the authority to fix the compensation of directors.

(i) **[Telephone board meetings]** Unless otherwise restricted by the charter or bylaws, members of the board or any committee may participate in a board/committee meeting by means of conference telephone or other communications equipment by means of which all persons participating in the meeting can hear each other, and such participation shall constitute presence in person at the meeting.

(j) **[No-stock corporations]** The charter of any nonstock corporation may provide for rules different from those in this section. To the extent it does not, this section applies and all references to the board, its members, and to stockholders shall be deemed to refer to the governing body of the corporation, its members, and the members of the corporation, respectively; and all references to shares thereof shall be deemed to refer to memberships and membership interests.

(k) **[Removal of directors]** "Any director or the entire board may be removed, **with or without cause**, by the holders of a majority of the shares then entitled to vote at an election of directors, **except** in the case of a corporation having:

    (1) **staggered or classified board** as provided in subsection (d): Unless the charter otherwise provides, shareholders may effect such removal **only for cause**; or

    (2) **cumulative voting**: If less than the entire board is to be removed, no director may be removed without cause if the votes cast against such director's removal would be sufficient to elect such director if then cumulatively voted at an election of the entire board of directors, or, if there be classes of directors, at an election of the class of directors of which such director is a part.

    Whenever the holders of any class or series are entitled to elect 1 or more directors by the charter, this subsection shall apply, in respect to the removal *without* cause of director(s) so elected, to the vote of that class or series and not to the vote of the outstanding shares as a whole.

§ 142. Officers; titles, duties, selection, term; failure to elect; vacancies.

(a) Every corporation shall have such officers with such titles and duties as stated in the bylaws or in a board resolution and as may be necessary to enable it to sign instruments and stock certificates which comply with §§ 103(a)(2) and 158. One of the officers shall have the duty to record the proceedings of the meetings of the stockholders and directors in a book to be kept for that purpose. Any number of offices may be held by the same person unless the charter or bylaws provide otherwise.

(b) The selection and terms of officers shall be prescribed by the bylaws or determined by the board or other governing body. Each officer holds office until his/her replacement, resignation, or removal. Any officer may resign at any time upon written notice to the corporation.

(c) "The corporation may secure the fidelity of any or all of its officers or agents by bond or otherwise."

(d) A failure to elect officers shall not dissolve or otherwise affect the corporation.

(e) Any vacancy shall be filled as the bylaws provide. In the absence of such provision, the vacancy shall be filled by the board of directors or other governing body.

§ 143. Loans to employees and officers; guaranty of obligations of employees and officers.

A corporation may lend money to or otherwise assist any employee, including an employee who is an officer or director, whenever, in the judgment of the directors, such loan or assistance may reasonably be expected to benefit the corporation. The loan etc. can take any form, including being interest-free or secured by a pledge of the corporation's own shares.

§ 144. Interested directors; quorum.

(a) No transaction between the corporation and any of its directors or officers (D/O), or any organization in which its D/O have a financial interest or serve as D/O, shall be void or voidable *solely for this reason,* or *solely* because the director or officer is present at or participates or votes in the meeting of the board or committee which authorizes the transaction, if

the transaction is approved in good faith after full *disclosure* by a majority vote

(1) of the disinterested directors or (2) of the shareholders; *or*

(3) **the transaction is *fair*** as to the corporation as of the time it is authorized, approved or ratified, by the board, a committee or the shareholders.

(b) Common or interested directors may be counted in determining the presence of a *quorum* at a meeting of the board or a committee which authorizes the contract or transaction.

§ 145. Indemnification of officers, directors, employees and agents; insurance.

This section applies to **any proceeding** to which a person is a party, or **any liability** to which a person is subject, by reason of the fact that the person is or was a director, officer, employee or agent of the corporation, or, at the request of the corporation, of another enterprise, including employee benefit plans.

(a) [*Power* to indemnify in third-party suits]   In connection with any proceeding other than an action by or in the right of the corporation, a corporation has power to indemnify against

reasonable **expenses** (including attorneys' fees), **judgments, fines** and **amounts paid in settlement**

if the person acted in good faith and, with respect to any *criminal* action or proceeding, had no reasonable cause to believe the person's conduct was unlawful (the termination of the proceeding by judgment etc. shall not, of itself, create a presumption of bad faith or reasonable cause, except on a guilty plea).

(b) [*Power* to indemnify in derivative actions]   In connection with an action by or in the right of the corporation, a corporation has power to indemnify against

reasonable **expenses** (including attorneys' fees)

if the person acted in good faith and has not been adjudged liable to the corporation (however, upon application the Court of Chancery or the court in which the action was brought can decide that, and how much, indemnification is fair and reasonable in spite of the finding of liability).

(c) [*Obligation* **to indemnify in case of successful defense**] To the extent that its present or former director or officer has been ~~successful on the~~ **merits or otherwise** in defense of any proceeding or any matter therein, the corporation **must reimburse** reasonable expenses (including attorneys' fees).

Warning: The legal texts presented here have been altered. Do not rely on them for legal advice

(d) **[Decision to indemnify: who, how]** "Any indemnification under subsections (a) and (b) of this section (unless ordered by a court) shall be made by the corporation only as authorized in the specific case upon a determination that indemnification is proper in the circumstances because the person has met the applicable standard of conduct set forth in subsections (a) and (b) of this section."

With respect to a current director or officer, such determination shall be made "(1) by a majority vote of the directors who are not parties to such action, suit or proceeding, even though less than a quorum, or (2) by a committee of such directors designated by majority vote of such directors, even though less than a quorum, or (3) if there are no such directors, or if such directors so direct, by independent legal counsel in a written opinion, or (4) by the stockholders."

(e) **[Advances]** The corporation *may* **pay expenses** (including attorneys' fees) **in advance** of the final disposition of the proceeding. Current officers or directors may be paid advances only upon undertaking to repay such amount if it shall ultimately be determined that he/she is not entitled to indemnification.

(f) **[Other rights to indemnification]** Indemnification and advances under this section's subsections are **not exclusive** of any other **rights** to indemnification or advances under any bylaw, agreement, vote of stockholders or disinterested directors or otherwise.

[no post facto amendments] A right to indemnification or advances under the charter or bylaws shall not be impaired by an amendment after the occurrence of the act or omission that is the subject of the action in question, unless such amendment had been explicitly reserved in the charter or bylaws, as the case may be.

(g) **[Power to maintain D&O insurance]** A corporation has **power** to purchase *insurance* on behalf of any person, and against any liability, covered by this section, **whether or not the corporation would have the power to** *indemnify.*

(h) **[Indemnification after merger]** For purposes of this section, after a consolidation or merger, directors, officers, employees and agents of a constituent corporation stand in the same position with respect to the resulting or surviving corporation as they would have with respect to such constituent corporation if its separate existence had continued.

(i) **[Employee benefit plans]**   With respect to employee benefit plans, references to "fines" shall include any excise taxes assessed; and acting in good faith includes acting in the interest of the participants and beneficiaries of an employee benefit plan.

(j) **[Former directors etc.; heirs and successors]**   "The indemnification and advancement of expenses provided by, or granted pursuant to, this section shall, unless otherwise provided when authorized or ratified, continue as to a person who has ceased to be a director, officer, employee or agent and shall inure to the benefit of the heirs, executors and administrators of such a person."

(k) **[Exclusive jurisdiction of the Court of Chancery]**   The Court of Chancery has **exclusive** jurisdiction to hear and determine **all** actions for advancement of expenses or indemnification, whether brought under this section or otherwise. It may summarily determine a corporation's obligation to advance expenses (including attorneys' fees).

§ 146. Submission of matters for stockholder vote.

"A corporation may agree [= contractually bind itself] to submit a matter to a vote of its stockholders whether or not the board of directors determines at any time subsequent to approving such matter that such matter is no longer advisable and recommends that the stockholders reject or vote against the matter."

SUBCHAPTER V. STOCK AND DIVIDENDS

§ 151. Classes and series of stock; redemption; rights.

(a) **[Types and rights of stock]**   Every corporation may issue such classes and series of stock, with or without par value, and with such voting

[handwritten: Whatever put in the Charter is ok]

powers, designations, preferences, special rights, and qualifications thereof (= "rights") *as stated in the charter,* or in the board resolution(s) providing for the issue of such stock pursuant to authority expressly granted by the charter (= "issuing resolution").

Any of the rights of any such class or series may be made dependent upon facts ascertainable outside the charter or the issuing resolution, respectively, provided that the manner in which such facts shall operate upon the rights is clearly and explicitly set forth therein. The term "facts," as used in this subsection, includes the occurrence of any event, including a determination or action by any person or body, including the corporation.

The power to increase or decrease or otherwise adjust the capital stock as provided in this chapter shall apply to all or any such classes of stock.

(b) **[Redemption]** Any stock may be made redeemable by the corporation at its option or at the option of the stockholder or upon the happening of a specified event, and for such consideration as provided in the charter or the issuing resolution; provided however, that immediately following any such redemption 1 or more shares with full voting powers shall remain outstanding. Notwithstanding the limitation stated in the foregoing proviso:

(1) Any stock of a regulated investment company registered under the Investment Company Act of 1940 may be made subject to redemption by the corporation at its option or at the option of the stockholder.

(2) If a corporation holds (directly or indirectly) a license or franchise from a governmental agency to conduct its business or is a member of a national securities exchange, which license, franchise or membership is conditioned upon some or all of the stockholders possessing prescribed qualifications, then the stock may be made subject to redemption by the corporation to the extent necessary to prevent the loss of such license, franchise or membership or to reinstate it.

(c)/(d) **[Preferred or special stock]** The dividend © and liquidation (d) preferences of preferred or special stock are <u>determined by the charter or</u> the issuing resolution, as provided for in subsection (a).

(e) **[Conversion]** Any stock may be made convertible into, or exchangeable for, at the option of either the holder or the corporation or upon the happening of a specified event, other stock of the corporation, at such price(s) or rate(s) of exchange and with such adjustments as stated in the charter or in the issuing resolution.

(f) **[Certificated and uncertificated stock; rights and their explanation]** If a corporation is authorized to issue more than 1 class or series of stock, each **share certificate** shall contain on its face or back a full statement or a summary of the rights of the respective class or series or, except as

---

otherwise provided in § 202, a statement that the corporation will furnish such information without charge to each stockholder who so requests. For **uncertificated stock**, the information required to be set forth on certificates pursuant to the preceding sentence or § 156, 202(a), 218(a), or 364 shall be given in writing or by electronic transmission to the registered owner within a reasonable time after the issuance or transfer.

Except as otherwise expressly provided by law, the **rights and obligations of** the holders of **certificated and uncertificated stock** of the same class and series shall be **identical**.

(g) **[Procedure of, and status for, board resolutions designating share rights]** When the rights of shares are determined by board resolution, as permitted by the charter, or if such board-determined rights are changed by board resolution, as authorized by this subsection, a certificate of designations setting forth the resolution, and the number, class and series of shares to which it applies, shall be acknowledged and filed in accordance with § 103. The certificate of designation has the **effect of amending the charter**, except that it shall not prohibit the board from subsequently adopting such resolutions as authorized by this subsection.

Unless otherwise provided in the charter, if no shares have been issued of a class or series established by a board resolution, the board may amend the rights. When no shares of any such class or series are outstanding, the board may eliminate the certificate of designation determining the rights.

Unless otherwise provided in any such resolution, the number of shares to which such resolution applies may be increased (but not above the total number of authorized shares of the class) or decreased (but not below the number of shares thereof then outstanding) by the board. In case of a decrease, the number of shares so specified in the certificate shall resume the status which they had prior to the adoption of the first resolution.

§ 152. Issuance of stock; lawful consideration; fully paid stock.

The consideration, as determined pursuant to § 153(a)/(b), for newly issued shares may consist of any benefit to the corporation, and shall be paid in such form and in such manner, as the board shall determine. The board resolution authorizing the issue must at least specify

- the maximum number of shares and the time period during which they may be issued;
- a manner to determine the number of, and times at which, shares are to be issued (which may include a determination or action by any person or body, including the corporation); and
- a formula to determine the minimum amount of consideration. The formula may depend upon facts ascertainable outside the formula, provided the manner in which such facts shall operate upon the formula is clearly and expressly specified.

In the absence of actual fraud in the transaction, the board's judgment as to the consideration's value is conclusive. The shares are deemed fully paid and nonassessable upon receipt by the corporation of such consideration, subject to § 156.

§ 153. Consideration for stock.

(a) Par-value shares may be issued for such consideration, having a value not less than the par value thereof, as determined from time to time by the board, or by the stockholders if the charter so provides.

(b) No-par shares may be issued for such consideration as is determined from time to time by the board, or by the stockholders if the charter so provides.

(c) Treasury shares may be disposed of by the corporation for such consideration as may be determined from time to time by the board, or by the stockholders if the charter so provides.

(d) If the charter reserves to the stockholders the right to determine the consideration for the issue of any shares, the stockholders shall, unless the certificate requires a greater vote, do so by a vote of a majority of the outstanding stock entitled to vote thereon.

§ 154. Determination of amount of capital; capital, surplus and net assets defined.

For each issue of shares of capital stock, the board may specify that only part of the consideration received shall be **capital.** The board shall specify that amount in dollars. That amount shall be in excess of the aggregate par value, if any, of the shares issued. If no such board resolution is adopted (1) in a cash issue, at the time of issue, or (2) in an issue for consideration other than cash, within 60 days after the issue, then the amount of consideration alloted to capital shall be (a) in an issue of no-par stock, the full consideration, and (b) in an issue of par-value stock, its aggregate par value. In respect of any shares without par value, the amount of consideration so determined to be capital shall be the **stated capital** of such shares.

The excess, if any, at any given time, of the corporation's net assets over the amount so determined to be capital shall be **surplus. Net assets** means the amount by which total assets exceed total liabilities.

The board may from time to time increase the corporation's capital by transfering to the capital account a portion of the surplus. The board may allocate the additional capital to any shares of any designated class.

For purposes of this section and §§ 160 and 170, the capital of any nonstock corporation shall be zero.

§ 155. Fractions of shares.

A corporation may issue fractions of a share. If not, it shall (1) arrange for the disposition of fractional interests by those entitled thereto, (2) pay in cash their fair value as of the time when those entitled to receive such fractions are determined or (3) issue scrip or warrants in registered or bearer form entitling the holder to receive a full share upon the surrender of such scrip or warrants aggregating a full share. Fractional shares, but not scrip or warrants unless otherwise provided therein, carry voting, dividend, and liquidation rights. Scrip or warrants may be issued subject to any conditions; in particular, they may be made subject to forfeiture if not exchanged for full shares before a specified date.

§ 156. Partly paid shares.

All or part of a corporation's shares may be issued as partly paid and subject to call for the remainder of the consideration. Each corresponding stock certificate, or the corporation's records in the case of uncertificated shares, shall state the paid and total amounts of the consideration due. Dividends upon partly paid shares are reduced in proportion to the part of consideration still outstanding.

§ 157. Rights and options respecting stock.

(a) Subject to the provisions of the charter, a corporation may <u>create and issue</u> <u>rights or options to acquire from the corporation shares of its capital stock</u>

("warrants"). The warrants shall be evidenced by or in such document(s) as determined by the board.

(b) The terms of exercise of the warrants (including any formula to determine the exercise price) are determined by the charter, or in the board resolution providing for their creation and issue. They shall be set forth or incorporated by reference in the instrument(s) evidencing the warrants. Any formula may depend upon facts ascertainable outside the formula, provided the manner in which such facts shall operate upon the formula is clearly and expressly specified. In the absence of actual fraud in the transaction, the directors' judgment as to the sufficiency of the consideration for the issuance of the warrants shall be conclusive.

(c) The board may authorize 1 or more officers to: (i) designate other officers and employees of the corporation or of any of its subsidiaries as recipients of warrants, and/or (ii) determine the number of warrants they shall receive. The board resolution shall specify the total number of warrants such officer(s) may so award.

(d) The exercise price of warrants to acquire par-value shares shall be no less than the shares' par value. The exercise price of warrants to acquire no-par shares shall be determined in the manner provided in § 153.

§ 158. Stock certificates; uncertificated shares.

Shares shall be represented by certificates, except that the board may resolve that some or all shares shall be uncertificated. Such resolution shall not apply to shares represented by a certificate until such certificate is surrendered to the corporation.

Every holder of certificated stock is entitled to have a certificate representing the number of shares registered. The certificate shall be signed by, or in the name of, the corporation by any two authorized officers of the corporation. Signatures may be a facsimile. Signatures are valid even if any officer, transfer agent or registrar who has signed ceases to be such officer, transfer agent or registrar before the certificate is issued.

A corporation shall **not** have power to issue a certificate in **bearer** form.

§ 159. Shares of stock; personal property, transfer and taxation.

Shares are deemed **personal property** and transferable as provided in Article 8 – Investment Securities – of the Uniform Commercial Code.

Warning: The legal texts presented here have been altered. Do not rely on them for legal advice

Delaware does **not tax** stocks or bonds owned by **non-residents** or by foreign corporations.

Transfers of shares made for collateral security, and not absolutely, shall be so expressed in the share register's entry of transfer if both transferor and transferee request the corporation to do so when they request the transfer.

§ 160. Corporation's powers respecting ownership, voting, etc., of its own stock; rights of stock called for redemption.

(a) Every corporation may own, and deal in and with, **its own shares; except** that:

    (1) When the **capital** of the corporation is **impaired**, or would become impaired by the transaction, a nonstock corporation may not purchase or redeem its own shares for cash or other property; a stock corporation may only do so if such shares will be retired upon their acquisition and the capital of the corporation reduced in accordance with §§ 243 and 244 (ordinary shares can be so acquired and retired only if no preferred shares remain outstanding). The foregoing does not affect a corporation's obligation given as consideration for its acquisition of its shares at a time when its capital was not impaired and did not thereby become impaired.

    (2) If the corporation has the **option to redeem** certain shares, it may not purchase them for more than their redemption price.

    (3) **Redemption** is possible only in accordance with

        a.   for stock corporations, § 151 (b) and the charter;

        b.   for nonstock corporations, the charter.

(b) Nothing in this section affects a corporation's right to resell any of its shares theretofore purchased or redeemed out of surplus and which have not been retired, for such consideration as shall be fixed by the board.

(c) Shares of its **own capital stock** belonging to the corporation shall **neither** be **entitled to vote nor** be **counted for quorum purposes**; this includes shares belonging to another corporation, if a majority of the shares entitled to vote in the election of directors of such other corporation is held, directly or indirectly, by the corporation. The foregoing does not apply to stock held by the corporation in a fiduciary capacity.

(d) Shares **called for redemption** are deemed not outstanding for the purpose of voting or determining the total number of shares entitled to vote on and after the date on which written notice of redemption has been sent to holders thereof and a sum sufficient to redeem such shares has been irrevocably deposited or set aside to pay the redemption price upon surrender of certificates.

§ 161. Issuance of additional stock; when and by whom.

The **directors** may **at any time** issue or take subscriptions for additional shares up to the amount authorized in the corporation's charter.

§ 162. Liability of stockholder or subscriber for stock not paid in full.

(a) A **holder** of or **subscriber** for a share is **bound to pay any unpaid balance** of the issue or subscription price if the other assets of the corporation are insufficient to satisfy the claims of its creditors.

(b) The amounts payable under (a) may be recovered as provided in § 325, after a writ of execution against the corporation has been returned unsatisfied as provided in said § 325.

(c) "Any person becoming an **assignee or transferee** of shares or of a subscription for shares **in good faith** and without knowledge or notice that the full consideration therefor has not been paid shall **not** be personally **liable** for any unpaid portion of such consideration, but the transferor shall remain liable therefor."

(d) Liability as a stockholder does not fall onto any person holding shares as collateral security or as a fiduciary, but it does fall onto the person pledging such shares or the funds held in such fiduciary capacity, respectively.

(e) "No liability under this section or under § 325 shall be asserted more than 6 years after the issuance of the stock or the date of the subscription upon which the assessment is sought."

(f) "In any action by a receiver or trustee of an insolvent corporation or by a judgment creditor to obtain an assessment under this section, any stockholder or subscriber for stock of the insolvent corporation may appear and contest the claim or claims of such receiver or trustee."

---

§ 163. Payment for stock not paid in full.

The stock shall be paid for in such amounts and at such times as the directors may require. The directors may, from time to time, demand payment, in respect of each share not fully paid, of such sum of money as the necessities of the business may, in the judgment of the board, require, not exceeding in the whole the balance remaining unpaid. The directors shall mail written notice at least 30 days before payment to the last known post-office address of each holder of or subscriber for stock which is not fully paid.

§ 164. Failure to pay for stock; remedies.

The directors may collect any due and unpaid amount by an action at law (which may be brought within the county where the corporation has its registered office), or they shall sell at public sale such part of the shares of the delinquent stockholder as will pay all demands then due from such stockholder with interest and all incidental expenses.

Notice of the time and place of such sale and of the sum due on each share shall be

- given by advertisement at least 1 week before the sale, in a newspaper in the county of this State where such corporation's registered office is located
- mailed to the delinquent stockholder at his last known post-office address, at least 20 days before the sale.

If the amount due cannot be obtained in the public sale, nor by an action at law within 1 year from the bringing of such action, the stock and any partial consideration previously paid for it is forfeited to the corporation.

§ 165. Revocability of preincorporation subscriptions.

A subscription for stock of a corporation to be formed shall be irrevocable for a period of 6 months from its date, except with the consent of all other subscribers or of the corporation and unless otherwise provided by the terms of the subscription.

§ 166. Formalities required of stock subscriptions.

A subscription for stock of a corporation is enforceable against a subscriber only if it is in writing and signed by the subscriber or her agent.

§ 167. Lost, stolen or destroyed stock certificates; issuance of new certificate or uncertificated shares.

A corporation may issue a new certificate of stock or uncertificated shares in place of any certificate allegedly lost, stolen or destroyed ("replacement shares"); and the corporation may require from the owner a bond sufficient to indemnify the corporation against any claim related thereto.

§ 168. Judicial proceedings to compel issuance of new certificate or uncertificated shares.

(a) If a corporation refuses to issue replacement shares [see § 167], the owner may apply to the Court of Chancery for an order requiring the corporation to show cause why it should not issue them. The complaint shall state the name of the corporation, the number and date of the certificate (if known or ascertainable by the plaintiff), the number of shares represented thereby and to whom issued, and the circumstances attending its loss, theft or destruction. Thereupon the court shall make the order requiring the corporation to show cause at a time and place therein designated. A copy of the complaint and order shall be served upon the corporation at least 5 days before the time designated in the order.

(b) If, upon hearing, the court is satisfied that

- the plaintiff is the lawful owner of the number of shares, or any part thereof, described in the complaint,
- the certificate therefor has been lost, stolen or destroyed, and
- no sufficient cause has been shown why replacement shares should not be issued, it shall make an order requiring the corporation to issue and deliver to the plaintiff replacement shares. In its order the court shall direct that the plaintiff give the corporation a bond in such form and with such security as to the court appears sufficient to indemnify the corporation against any claim that may be made against it in relation with the issue of the replacement shares. The corporation's liability shall be limited to the amount specified in such bond.

§ 169. Situs of ownership of stock.

For all purposes except taxation, the situs of the ownership of the shares of any Delaware corporation shall be regarded as in this State.

§ 170. Dividends; payment; wasting asset corporations.

(a) The **directors**, subject to any restrictions in the charter, may declare and pay dividends upon the shares, **either**

   (1) **out of the corporation's surplus**, as defined in §§ 154 and 244, **or**

   (2) if there is no such surplus, **out of its net profits** for the fiscal year in which the dividend is declared and/or the preceding fiscal year.

No dividend shall be declared or paid while the corporation's capital, computed in accordance with §§ 154 and 244, is less than the capital represented by all outstanding shares having a preference upon the distribution of assets.

The foregoing does not affect a corporation's obligation given as dividend at a time when the corporation could lawfully declare and pay dividends, nor any payments made on such obligation.

(b) Subject to any restrictions in the charter, the directors of any corporation engaged in the exploitation of wasting assets (including the exploitation of natural resources or patents, or primarily the liquidation of specific assets) may determine the net profits therefrom without taking into consideration the depletion of such assets resulting from lapse of time, consumption, liquidation or exploitation.

§ 171. Special purpose reserves.

The directors may set apart out of any funds available for dividends reserve(s) for any proper purpose and may abolish any such reserve(s).

§ 172. Liability of directors and committee members as to dividends or stock redemption.

In determining the existence and amount of funds properly available for distribution by way of dividends, share repurchases or share redemption, a director is protected by § 141(e) (reliance on expert opinions etc).

§ 173. Declaration and payment of dividends.

No corporation shall pay dividends except in accordance with this chapter.

Dividends may be paid in cash, in property, or in shares of the corporation.

If the dividend is to be paid in theretofore unissued shares of the corporation, the board shall designate a corresponding amount of capital, which must not be less than the aggregate par value, if any, of the shares paid as dividends. Such designation is unnecessary if shares are being distributed by a corporation pursuant to a split-up or division of its stock rather than as a dividend paid in stock.

§ 174. Liability of directors for unlawful payment of dividend or unlawful stock purchase or redemption; exoneration from liability; contribution among directors; subrogation.

(a) Within 6 years of any wilful or negligent violation of § 160 (illegal share purchase or redemption) or 173 (illegal dividend), the directors under whose administration the same may happen shall be jointly and severally liable to the corporation, and to its creditors in the event of its dissolution or insolvency, to the full amount unlawfully paid, with interest.

Any director absent or dissenting from the act or resolution by which the same was done, may avoid liability by causing her dissent to be entered on the books containing the minutes of the proceedings of the directors at the time the same was done, or immediately after such director has notice of the same.

((b)/(c)) Any director against whom a claim is successfully asserted under this section shall be entitled …

(b) … to contribution from the other directors who voted for or concurred in the unlawful dividend, stock purchase or stock redemption; and

(c) … to be subrogated to the rights of the corporation against stockholders who received the dividends etc. with knowledge of facts indicating that such payment was unlawful under this chapter, in proportion to the amounts received by such stockholders respectively.

SUBCHAPTER VI. STOCK TRANSFERS

§ 201. Transfer of stock, stock certificates and uncertificated stock.

Article 8 – Investment Securities – of the Uniform Commercial Code governs the transfer of stock and the stock certificates, except as otherwise provided in, or inconsistent with, this chapter.

§ 202. Restrictions on transfer and ownership of securities.

A restriction on the transfer of securities of a corporation, or on the amount of a corporation's securities that may be owned by any person or group, is …

(a) ... enforceable against

- a person with actual knowledge of the restriction, and
- *anybody* if the restriction is noted conspicuously on the certificate(s) representing the restricted securities or, in the case of uncertificated shares, contained in the notice(s) given pursuant to § 151(f).

(b) ... **imposable** by the charter, the bylaws, or an agreement among any number of security holders or among such holders and the corporation. Securities issued prior to the adoption of the restriction are bound by it only if their holders are parties to an agreement or voted in favor of the restriction.

(c)/(e) ... **permitted** if it is lawful, in particular if it:

(1) obligates the holder of the restricted securities to offer to someone "a prior opportunity, to be exercised within a reasonable time, to acquire the restricted securities;"

(2) obligates someone "to purchase the securities which are the subject of an agreement respecting the purchase and sale of the restricted securities;"

(3) requires the corporation or the holders of any class or series of securities of the corporation to consent to any proposed transfer or transferee of the restricted securities, or to approve the amount of securities of the corporation that may be owned by any person or group of persons;

(4) obligates the holder of the restricted securities to sell or transfer an amount of restricted securities to someone, or causes or results in the automatic sale or transfer of an amount of restricted securities to someone; or

(5) prohibits or restricts the transfer of the restricted securities to, or their ownership by, designated persons or classes of persons, and such designation is not manifestly unreasonable.

(d) ... conclusively presumed to be for a reasonable purpose if it is for the purpose of maintaining any ...

(1) ... tax advantage (local, state, federal or foreign) to the corporation or its stockholders, including:

    a. the corporation's status as an S-corporation, or

    b. any tax attribute (including net operating losses),

    c. the qualification of the corporation as a real estate investment trust pursuant to the US Internal Revenue Code or regulations adopted thereunder, or

(2) … statutory or regulatory advantage or complying with any statutory or regulatory requirements under applicable local, state, federal or foreign law.

§ 203. Business combinations with interested stockholders.

(a) A corporation shall not engage in any business combination with any stockholder for a period of 3 years following the time that such stockholder ("the interested stockholder") came to own at least 15% of the outstanding voting stock of the corporation ("the acquisition"), except if:

    (1) The *board* had approved the *acquisition* prior to its consummation;

    (2) The interested stockholder owned at least 85% of the outstanding[1] voting stock upon consummation of the acquisition, **or**

    (3) The *business combination* is approved by the board, *and* by a 2/3 majority vote of the *other* stockholders in a meeting (i.e., not by written consent).

(b) Subsection (a) shall not apply if at the time[2] of the acquisition:

    (1)/(3) **[opt-out]** The corporation's charter or shareholder-approved bylaws contain a provision expressly electing not to be governed by this section (however, an amendment of this type becomes effective only 12 months after its adoption, unless the corporation has always met paragraph (4) below and has not affirmatively elected in its charter to be governed by this section);

---

[1] Shares owned by executive directors or employee stock plans are not counted for purposes of determining the voting stock outstanding (however, shares owned by employee stock plans are counted if the employee participants have the right to determine confidentially whether their shares held subject to the plan will be tendered in a tender or exchange offer).

[2] [The timing requirement follows, inter alia, from subsubsection (7) and the closing proviso of subsection (b).]

Warning: The legal texts presented here have been altered. Do not rely on them for legal advice

(4) **[closely held corporations; no opt-in]** The corporation does not have a class of voting stock that is: (i) Listed on a national securities exchange; or (ii) held of record by more than 2,000 stockholders, and the charter does not contain an election to be governed by this section; or

(5) **[inadvertent acquisition]** A stockholder becomes an interested stockholder only inadvertently and divests as soon as practicable.

Subsection (a) also does not apply if:

(6) **[competing board-approved transaction]** The business combination is proposed between the announcement[3] and the consummation or abandonment of a takeover[4] of the corporation by a third party, if such takeover is

- by a person who either was not an interested stockholder during the previous three years or who became an interested stockholder with the approval of the board or with the benefit of the exemptions in sub-subsections (1)-(4); and
- not opposed by a majority of those board members who were directors prior to *any* person becoming an interested stockholder during the previous 3 years or were recommended for election or elected to succeed such directors by a majority of such directors.

(c) As used in this section only, the term:

(3) "Business combination" means:

(i) Any merger or consolidation of the corporation *with the interested stockholder*;

(ii) Any disposition *to the interested stockholder* of assets of the corporation with an aggregate market value equal to 10% or more of the corporation's assets or of all its outstanding stock;

---

[3] This means the earlier of the public announcement or of the following: The corporation must give at least 20 days' notice to all interested stockholders prior to the consummation of any merger or asset disposition described in the next footnote.

[4] This means a merger of the corporation (except a merger for which pursuant to § 251(f) no vote of the corporation's stockholders is required), a disposition of at least 50% of the corporation's assets (including assets of any direct or indirect majority-owned subsidiary), or a tender offer for at least 50% of the corporation's shares

Warning: The legal texts presented here have been altered. Do not rely on them for legal advice

(iii)/(iv) Any transaction which results in an increase of the interested stockholders' share of the stock of the corporation;

(v) Any receipt by the interested stockholder of any financial benefit, directly or indirectly (except proportionately as a stockholder of such corporation) by or through the corporation;

including in each case a transaction with any direct or indirect majority-owned subsidiary of the corporation.

(5) "Interested stockholder" means any person who owns at least 15% of the outstanding voting stock of the corporation, or who owned such 15% at any time during the previous three years and presently holds the power to direct management or a position as director or officer of the corporation.[5]

(9) "Ownership of stock", "own", etc. of a corporation's stock by a person means not only beneficial direct or indirect ownership by the person itself, but also

- any right to acquire or vote such stock; except the mere receipt of

  – stock tendered pursuant to a tender/exchange offer before it is accepted for purchase/exchange;
  – revocable proxies/consents given in response to a proxy/consent solicitation made to 10 or more persons;

- ownership through or with other persons

  – which are controlled by, or under common control with, or controlling, the person;[6]
  – of which the person owns, directly or indirectly, 20% or more of any class of voting stock;
  – in which the person is a director, officer, or partner;
  – who are relatives of the person with the same residence; or

---

[5] Provided, however, that a person is not an interested stockholder if its ownership in excess of 15% came about solely through action of the corporation, and such person did not subsequently acquire additional shares.

[6] Control can be direct or indirect and means the power to direct the management and policies of a person. A person who is the owner of 20% or more of the outstanding voting stock of any entity shall be presumed to have control of such entity, in the absence of proof to the contrary.

Warning: The legal texts presented here have been altered. Do not rely on them for legal advice

- who are trusts in which the person is the trustee or at least a 20% beneficiary.

(d) No provision of a charter or bylaw shall require, for any vote of stockholders required by this section, a greater vote of stockholders than that specified in this section.

(e) The Court of Chancery is hereby vested with *exclusive* jurisdiction to hear and determine all matters with respect to this section.

§ 204. Ratification of defective corporate acts and stock [OMITTED]

§ 205. Proceedings regarding validity of defective corporate acts and stock [OMITTED]

SUBCHAPTER VII. MEETINGS, ELECTIONS, VOTING AND NOTICE

§ 211. Meetings of stockholders.

(a)(1) **[place]** Unless the charter or bylaws designate a place, the board determines where to hold a stockholder meeting, including the possibility to hold a meeting solely by means of remote communication (cf. paragraph (2)).

(2) **[remote communication]** If and subject to any rules authorized by the board, stockholders and proxyholders not physically present at a stockholder meeting may, by means of remote communication:

a. Participate in the meeting; and

b. Be deemed present in person and vote, provided that the corporation shall implement reasonable measures

(i) to verify that such person is a stockholder or proxyholder and

(ii) to provide such person a reasonable opportunity to participate and to vote, including an opportunity to read or hear the proceedings of the meeting substantially concurrently with such proceedings, and

(iii) maintain a record of any action taken by such person at the meeting.

(b) **[Annual meeting]** An annual meeting of stockholders shall be held for the election of directors and any other proper business on a date and at a time designated by or in the manner provided in the bylaws.

[Written consent in lieu of an annual meeting] Notwithstanding the foregoing, no annual meeting is required if directors are elected by action by written consent and

- this consent is unanimous, or
- all of the directorships to which directors could be elected at an annual meeting held at the effective time of such action are vacant and are filled by the action.

(c) **[failure to hold annual meeting]** "A failure to hold the annual meeting at the designated time or to elect a sufficient number of directors to conduct the business of the corporation shall **not affect otherwise valid corporate acts** or work a forfeiture or dissolution of the corporation except as may be otherwise specifically provided in this chapter."

If the annual meeting is not held on the designated date and no action by written consent in lieu of an annual meeting has been taken, the **directors shall cause** the meeting to be held as soon as is convenient.

If the delay exceeds 30 days, or if no date has been designated and 13 months have passed since the last annual meeting (or written consent in lieu thereof, or organization of the corporation), the **Court of Chancery may summarily order** a meeting upon the application of any stockholder or director. No quorum requirement applies to such meeting. The Court of Chancery may issue such orders as may be appropriate, including designating the time and place, record date, or form of notice for such meeting.

(d) **[Special meetings]** Special meetings of stockholders may be called by the board or by persons authorized by the charter or bylaws.

(e) **[Form of ballot for director elections]** Unless otherwise provided in the charter, all elections of directors shall be by written ballot, except that the board may authorize electronic transmission if such transmission allows determination that it was authorized by the stockholder or proxy holder.

§ 212. Voting rights of stockholders; proxies; limitations.

(a) **[Votes per share]** Each share confers one vote, subject to §213. The charter may provide otherwise. in that case, every reference in this chapter to a proportion of shares shall refer to such proportion of the votes.

(b) **[Proxies allowed; duration]** Each stockholder with voting rights may authorize other person(s) to act for her by proxy. No proxy shall be acted upon after 3 years from its date, unless the proxy provides for a longer period.

(c) **[Non-exclusive forms of proxy]** Without limiting other forms, the following are valid proxies pursuant to subsection (b):

    (1) Written authorization executed by the stockholder or her agent by causing such person's signature to be affixed to such writing by any reasonable means including facsimile.

    (2) Electronic transmission (including telegram or cablegram) by, or authorized by, the stockholder to the proxy holder or its duly authorized agent if such transmission allows determination that it was authorized by the stockholder. Persons making that determination shall specify the information upon which they relied.

(d) **[Copies of proxy]** Any reliable and complete reproduction of the entire writing or transmission created pursuant to subsection © may be used in lieu of the original.

(e) **[Irrevocable proxy]** A proxy shall be irrevocable if it states so "and if, and only as long as, it is coupled with an interest sufficient in law to support an irrevocable power," be it an interest in the stock itself or an interest in the corporation generally.

§ 213. Fixing date for determination of stockholders of record.

(a) **[record date for meetings]** To determine the stockholders entitled to *notice* of any stockholder meeting, the board may by resolution fix a record date between 10 and 60 days before the meeting, but not earlier than the date of the resolution. Such date also determines *voting* rights unless the board concurrently fixes a later date on or before the date of the meeting for such determination. If the board does not fix one, the record date for notice and voting is the close of business on the day next preceding the day on which (i) notice is given or, (ii) if notice is waived, the meeting is held. A determination of stockholder notice and voting rights for a meeting also applies to any adjournment unless the board fixes new record dates for both in accordance with the foregoing provisions.

(b) **[record date for written consent]** To determine the stockholders entitled to consent to corporate action in writing without a meeting, the board may by resolution fix a record date between 0 and 10 days from the date of the resolution. If the board does not fix a record date, then

- if no prior action by the board is required by this chapter, the record date is the first date on which a signed written consent is delivered to the corporation;[7]
- if prior action by the board is required by this chapter, the record date is at the close of business on the day on which the board adopts the required resolution.

(c) **[record date for other lawful actions]** To determine the stockholders for the purpose of any other lawful action (e.g., receipt of a dividend, or exercise of conversion rights), the board may by resolution fix a record date not more than 60 days prior to such action and no earlier than the date of the resolution. If the board does not fix one, the record date for any such purpose shall be at the close of business on the day on which the board adopts the resolution relating thereto.

§ 214. Cumulative voting.

The charter may provide that at all or some elections of directors, each stockholder is entitled to as many votes as

- the number of votes which (except for such provision as to cumulative voting) such holder would be entitled to cast for the election of directors with respect to such holder's shares,

multiplied by

- the number of directors to be elected by such holder,

and that such holder may choose to cast all such votes for a single director or distribute them among several directors.

---

[7] By delivery to its registered office in this State, its principal place of business or an officer or agent of the corporation having custody of the book in which proceedings of meetings of stockholders are recorded. Delivery made to a corporation's registered office shall be by hand or by certified or registered mail, return receipt requested.

Warning: The legal texts presented here have been altered. Do not rely on them for legal advice

§ 215. Voting rights of members of nonstock corporations; quorum; proxies.

(a) **[limited application of §§ 211-16]** §§ 211 through 214 and 216 shall not apply to nonstock corporations, except for § 211(a) and (d) and § 212(c), (d), and (e).

(b) **[votes per member; proxies]** Each member of a nonstock corporation has one vote, unless otherwise provided in the charter or bylaws, and subject to subsection (f). Proxies are permitted, but no proxy shall be voted on after 3 years from its date, unless the proxy provides for a longer period.

(c) **[quorum and required vote]** Unless otherwise provided in this chapter, the charter or bylaws of a nonstock corporation may specify a quorum and required majority for any action of a meeting of members. In the absence of such specification,

    (1) 1/3 of the members constitute a quorum;

    (2) All matters other than the election of the governing body require the affirmative vote of a majority of members present in person or represented by proxy ("present") and entitled to vote on the matter, unless a greater majority is required by this chapter;

    (3) The election of members of the governing body requires a plurality of the votes of the members present and entitled to vote thereon; and

    (4) Where a separate vote by a class or group is required, a majority of members of such class or group constitutes a quorum, and all matters other than the election of the governing body require the affirmative vote of the majority of the class members present.

(d) **[failure to hold election]** "If the election of the governing body of any nonstock corporation is not held on the day designated by the bylaws, the governing body shall cause the election to be held as soon thereafter as convenient. The failure to hold such an election at the designated time shall not work any forfeiture or dissolution of the corporation, but the Court of Chancery may summarily order such an election to be held upon the application of any member of the corporation." No quorum requirement applies to such ordered election.

(e) **[electronic ballot]** If authorized by the governing body, any requirement of a written ballot shall be satisfied by electronic transmission if such transmission allows determination that it was authorized by the member or proxy holder.

(f) **[record date]** The record date for any meeting or corporate action is the date of such meeting or action, unless the charter, bylaws, or a resolution of the governing body provides another record date not earlier than the action by the governing body fixing such date.

§ 216. Quorum and required vote for stock corporations.

Subject to this chapter in respect of the vote that shall be required for a specified action, the charter or bylaws may specify the number of shares and/or other voting securities that constitute a quorum for, and the votes required for any action of, a stockholder meeting. The quorum must not be less than one-third of the shares entitled to vote at the meeting, or, where a separate vote by class or series is required, of the shares of that class or series. In the absence of such specification:

(1) A majority of the shares entitled to vote, present in person or represented by proxy ("present"), constitute a quorum;

(2) All matters other than the election of directors require the affirmative vote of the majority of shares present and entitled to vote on the subject matter,

(3) Directors are elected by a plurality of the votes of the shares present and entitled to vote on the election; and

(4) Where a separate vote by a class or series is required, a majority of shares of such class or series constitutes a quorum, and all matters other than the election of directors require the affirmative vote of the majority of that class's or series' shares present.

A bylaw amendment adopted by stockholders which specifies the votes necessary for the election of directors shall not be further amended by the board.

§ 217. Voting rights of fiduciaries, pledgors and joint owners of stock.

(a) **[fiduciaries; pledgors]** Persons holding stock in a fiduciary capacity are entitled to vote these shares. Pledged stock is represented and voted by the pledgor, unless the pledgor has expressly empowered the pledgee in the transfer on the books of the corporation.

(b) **[multiple record owners or fiduciaries]** If shares or other voting securities stand of record in the names of multiple persons ...,[8] or if multiple persons have the same fiduciary relationship respecting the same shares, their votes will be counted as provided in the instrument or order granting such powers if it is furnished to the secretary of the corporation.[9] Otherwise, (1)/(2) the vote of the majority binds all, but (3) if the vote is evenly split, it is counted proportionally unless the Court of Chancery or other court with jurisdiction appoints a tie-breaker upon application by one of the voting persons or by a beneficiary, if any.

§ 218. Voting trusts and other voting agreements.

(a)[10] **[voting trusts allowed]** Stockholders may by written agreement vest in one or more voting trustees the right to vote the stock for the duration, and subject to the terms and conditions, stated in such agreement.

[stock certificates] New certificates of stock or uncertificated stock representing the stock shall be issued to the voting trustee(s), and any outstanding certificates shall be surrendered and cancelled, after the delivery of a copy of the agreement to the corporation's registered office or principal place of business. The filed copy shall be open to the inspection of any stockholder or any trust beneficiary daily during business hours. The certificates and the corporation's stock ledger shall state that the certificates are issued pursuant to such agreement.

[proxy; liability limitation] The voting trustee(s) may vote the stock either in person or by proxy, and in so doing shall incur no responsibility as stockholder, trustee or otherwise, except for their own individual malfeasance.

(b) **[amendments to voting trusts]** Any amendment to a voting trust agreement shall be made by a written agreement, a copy of which shall be delivered to the corporation's registered office or principal place of business.

(c) **[voting agreements allowed]** Stockholders may by written agreement agree to exercise any voting rights as provided by the agreement.

---

[8] Examples include fiduciaries, members of a partnership, joint tenants, tenants in common, and tenants by the entirety.

[9] In particular, tenants have voting rights proportional to their interests.

[10] The final sentence of paragraph (a) is a less detailed copy of §217(b) and hence seems duplicative; it is omitted here.

(d) **[non-exclusivity]** "This section shall not be deemed to invalidate any voting or other agreement among stockholders or any irrevocable proxy which is not otherwise illegal."

§ 219. List of stockholders entitled to vote; penalty for refusal to produce; stock ledger.

(a) The corporation shall, at least 10 days in advance of any stockholder meeting, make a complete list of the stockholders entitled to vote thereat; if the record date is less than 10 days before the meeting, the list shall reflect the stockholders entitled to vote as of the tenth day before the meeting date. Stockholders shall appear in alphabetical order with their address and the number of shares registered in their name; email or other electronic contact information is not required.

Such list shall be **open to the examination of any stockholder** for any purpose germane to the meeting for a period of at least 10 days prior to the meeting:

(i) on a reasonably accessible electronic network, provided that the access information is provided with the notice of the meeting, or

(ii) during ordinary business hours, at the corporation's principal place of business.

It shall also be available to any stockholder during the entire meeting at the place of such meeting or, if the meeting is to be held solely by means of remote communication, on a reasonably accessible electronic network (access information shall be provided with the notice of the meeting).

If the corporation makes the list available on an electronic network, it may take reasonable steps to ensure that such information is available only to its stockholders.

(b) A stockholder may apply to the Court of Chancery for an order to compel the corporation to permit examination of the list. The burden of proof shall be on the corporation to establish that the stockholder seeks examination for a purpose not germane to the meeting. "The Court may summarily order the corporation to permit examination of the list upon such conditions as the Court may deem appropriate, and may make such additional orders as may be appropriate, including, without limitation, postponing the meeting or voiding the results of the meeting."

(c) "For purposes of this chapter, "stock ledger" means one or more records administered by or on behalf of the corporation in which the names of all of the corporation's stockholders of record, the address and number of shares registered in the name of each such stockholder, and all issuances and transfers of stock of the corporation are recorded in accordance with § 224 of this title. The stock ledger shall be the only evidence as to who are the stockholders entitled by this section to examine the list required by this section or to vote in person or by proxy at any meeting of stockholders."

§ 220. Inspection of books and records.

(a) As used in this section:

    (1) "Stockholder" means record or beneficial owner, including the beneficiary of a voting trust.

    (2) "Subsidiary" means any entity directly or indirectly owned (in whole or in part) and controlled by the corporation.

    (3) "Under oath" includes statements the declarant affirms to be true under penalty of perjury.

(b) [stockholder right to inspection] Any stockholder, in person or by agent, upon written demand under oath stating the purpose thereof, has the right during usual business hours to inspect for any purpose reasonably related to such person's interest as a stockholder ("proper purpose"), and to make copies and extracts from:

    (1) The corporation's stock ledger, a list of its stockholders, and its other **books and records**; and

    (2) A subsidiary's books and records, to the extent that:

        a. The corporation has actual possession and control of such records; or

        b. The corporation could obtain such records through the exercise of control over such subsidiary, provided that as of the date of the demand:

            1. The stockholder inspection would not constitute a breach of an agreement between the corporation or the subsidiary and a person not affiliated with the corporation; and

2. The subsidiary would not have the right under the law applicable to it to deny the corporation access to such books and records upon demand by the corporation.

The demand under oath shall be directed to the corporation at its registered office or principal place of business. Any demand by a beneficial owner shall state under oath the person's status as a stockholder, be accompanied by documentary evidence of beneficial ownership, and state that such documentary evidence is a true and correct copy of what it purports to be. Any demand by an agent shall be accompanied by a power of attorney.

(c) **[judicial enforcement of stockholder inspection rights]** If the corporation refuses the inspection or does not reply to the demand within 5 business days, the stockholder may apply to the Court of Chancery, which has exclusive jurisdiction to determine any right to inspection.

The stockholder shall first establish that such stockholder is a stockholder and has complied with the form and manner of making demand pursuant to paragraph (b). The burden of proof regarding proper purpose is on the corporation where the stockholder seeks to inspect the corporation's stock ledger or list of stockholders; for other books and records, it is on the stockholder.

The Court may award any relief it deems just and proper. In particular, it may summarily order the corporation to permit inspection etc., or to furnish to the stockholder a list of its stockholders as of a specific date on appropriate conditions, including that the stockholder first pay to the corporation the reasonable cost thereof.

(d) **[director right to inspection]** Any **director** shall have the right to examine the corporation's books and records for a purpose reasonably related to the director's position as a director. The Court of Chancery has exclusive jurisdiction to adjudicate such right and may award any relief it deems just and proper. The burden of proof regarding proper purpose is on the corporation.

§ 221. Voting, inspection and other rights of bondholders and debenture holders.

The charter may confer voting and other stockholder rights upon the holders of any obligations of the corporation. If the charter so provides, such obligations and their holders shall be deemed stock and stockholders, respectively, for the purpose of any provision of this chapter which requires the vote of stockholders, and the charter may divest the holders of capital stock, in whole or in part, of their right to vote on any corporate matter whatsoever, except as set forth in §242(b)(2).

§ 222. Notice of meetings and adjourned meetings.

(a) **[Notice required; content]** "Whenever stockholders are required or permitted to take any action at a meeting, a written notice of the meeting shall be given which shall state the place, if any, date and hour of the meeting, the means of remote communications, if any, by which stockholders and proxy holders may be deemed to be present in person and vote at such meeting, the record date for determining the stockholders entitled to vote at the meeting ["voting record date"], if such date is different from the record date for determining stockholders entitled to notice of the meeting ["notice record date"], and, in the case of a special meeting, the purpose or purposes for which the meeting is called."

(b) **[Time of notice]** Unless otherwise provided in this chapter, notice shall be given between 10 and 60 days (inclusive) before the meeting to each stockholder entitled to vote thereat as of the notice record date. If mailed, notice is given when deposited in the United States mail, postage prepaid, directed to the stockholder at such stockholder's address as it appears on the records of the corporation. An affidavit of an agent of the corporation that the notice has been given shall, in the absence of fraud, be prima facie evidence of the facts stated therein.

(c) **[Adjournments]** Notice need not be given of an adjourned meeting if the content required by paragraph (a) is announced at the original meeting, **unless**

- the bylaws require otherwise;
- the adjournment is for more than 30 days (in that case, notice shall be given to each stockholder entitled to vote at the meeting); or
- a new voting record date is fixed (in that case, a new notice record date shall be set).

At the adjourned meeting the corporation may transact any business which might have been transacted at the original meeting.

§ 223. Vacancies and newly created directorships.

(a) **[board power]** Unless otherwise provided in the charter or bylaws:

(1) Board vacancies, including newly created directorships, may be filled by a majority of the directors then in office, although less than a quorum; but

(2) if the charter entitles particular classes of stockholders to elect certain directorships, vacancies for such directorships may be filled by a majority of the directors elected by such class(es) then in office.

If a corporation has no directors in office, any officer or stockholder "may call a special meeting of stockholders in accordance with the charter or bylaws, or may apply to the Court of Chancery for a decree summarily ordering an election as provided in §211" or 215.

(b) **[staggered boards]** If the board is staggered, directors chosen under subsection (a) shall hold office until the next election of their class, and until their successors shall be elected and qualified.

(c) **[Chancery Court]** If, at the time of filling any vacancy, the directors then in office constitute less than a majority of the whole board (as constituted immediately prior to any such increase), the Court of Chancery may, upon application of stockholders holding at least 10 percent of the outstanding stock entitled to vote for such directors, summarily order an election for such directorship to be governed by § 211 or 215 as far as applicable.

(d) **[parting directors to elect their successors]** Unless otherwise provided in the charter or bylaws, directors resigning effective at a future date may participate in the election of their successors in accordance with subsection (a).

§ 224. Form of records.

A corporation may keep its records by any storage method, including distributed electronic networks, provided the records can be converted into clearly legible paper form within a reasonable time. This paper form

- shall be produced upon the request of any person entitled to inspect such records pursuant to any provision of this chapter, and
- is accepted for all purposes to the same extent as an original paper record would have been, provided the paper form accurately portrays the record.

---

§ 225. Contested election of directors; proceedings to determine validity.

(a) **[elections, resignations, etc.]** Upon application of any stockholder or director, or any officer whose title to office is contested, the Court of Chancery may determine the person entitled to an office of director or officer. The Court of Chancery may make any order as may be just and proper, including for notice, the production of records, and holding an election pursuant to § 211 or 215.

(b) **[other stockholder votes]** Upon application of any stockholder or of the corporation itself, the Court of Chancery may determine the result of any stockholder vote upon matters other than elections. No party besides the corporation need be joined.

(c) **[removal]** Upon application by the corporation or derivatively by a stockholder, the Court of Chancery may remove from office any director who has been

- convicted of a felony, or
- adjudicated by a court of competent jurisdiction to have breached the duty of loyalty,

in connection with the director's duties to the corporation, if the Court determines that the director did not act in good faith in performing the acts resulting in the prior conviction or judgment and judicial removal is necessary to avoid irreparable harm to the corporation. The Court may make necessary incidental orders.

(a)-(c) **[service; notice]** For purposes of the foregoing, service of the application upon the corporation's registered agent shall be deemed service upon the corporation and any persons whose title to office is contested. The registered agent shall immediately forward copies of the application in postpaid, sealed, registered letters to the corporation and these persons at their post-office addresses last known to the registered agent or furnished to the registered agent by the applicant stockholder. The Court may make such order respecting notice of such application as it deems proper.

§ 226. Appointment of custodian or receiver of corporation on deadlock or for other cause.

(a) The Court of Chancery, upon application of any stockholder, may appoint custodians or, if the corporation is insolvent, receivers for the corporation when:

    (1) The **stockholders are so divided** that they have failed to elect successors to directors whose terms have expired or would have expired upon qualification of their successors; or

    (2) The **directors are so divided** that the required vote for board action cannot be obtained, the stockholders are unable to terminate this division, and, as a result, the business of the corporation is threatened with irreparable injury; or

    (3) The corporation has abandoned its business and has failed within a reasonable time to take steps to dissolve, liquidate or distribute its assets.

(b) A custodian has all the powers and title of a receiver appointed under §291, but the custodian is to continue the business of the corporation rather than liquidate, except when the Court orders otherwise or in cases arising under paragraph (a)(3) or §352(a)(2).

(c) In the case of a charitable nonstock corporation, the applicant shall provide a copy of the application to the Attorney General within one week of its filing.

§ 227. Powers of Court in elections of directors.

In proceedings under §§ 211, 215 or 225, the Court of Chancery may (a) determine individuals' voting rights; (b) appoint a Master to hold any election; and punish any officer, director, or corporation for contempt (for a corporation, the maximum penalty is $5,000).

§ 228. Consent of stockholders or members in lieu of meeting.

(a)/(b) Unless otherwise provided in the charter, any action of a meeting of stockholders/member may be taken, without a meeting and prior notice, by signed written consent, delivered to the corporation, of stockholders/members having the minimum number of votes that would be necessary to take such action at a meeting at which all shares/members entitled to vote thereon were present and voted.[11]

(c) To be effective, sufficient written consents must be delivered to the corporation within 60 days of the delivery of the first written consent to the corporation.[12]

"Any person executing a consent may provide, whether through instruction to an agent or otherwise, that such a consent will be effective at a future time (including a time determined upon the happening of an event), no later than 60 days after such instruction is given or such provision is made, if evidence of such instruction or provision is provided to the corporation. Unless otherwise provided, any such consent shall be revocable prior to its becoming effective."

(d)(1) An electronic transmission (including telegram or cablegram) satisfies the requirements of subsection (a)/(b) if it contains sufficient information to determine (A) that it was transmitted by the stockholder/member or her authorized agent, and (B) the date of transmission. Delivery shall occur when a paper reproduction of the consent is delivered to the corporation.[13]

(2) Any reliable and complete reproduction of the entire written consent may be used in lieu of the original.

(e) Prompt notice of the action shall be given to non-consenting stockholders/members, if any, who would have been entitled to notice of the meeting if the action had been taken at a meeting and the notice record date had been the date that a sufficient number of written consents were first delivered to the corporation. If the action requires the filing of a certificate containing a statement concerning the vote, the certificate shall instead state that written consent has been given.

§ 229. Waiver of notice.

Any notice required by this chapter, the charter, or the bylaws ("required notice"), may be waived by the person entitled thereto in signed writing or by electronic transmission. Attendance of a meeting constitutes waiver of notice thereof, except attendance for the express purpose of objecting at the

---

[11] See note 7.

[12] The mode of delivery is subject to the preceding footnote.

[13] Id. Electronically transmitted consents may, however, be otherwise delivered to the corporation's principal place of business or the agent having custody of the minutes, if and to the extent a resolution of the board / governing body so provides.

Warning: The legal texts presented here have been altered. Do not rely on them for legal advice

beginning of the meeting, to the transaction of any business because the meeting is not lawfully called or convened. The waiver need not state the business or purpose of the meeting unless so required by the charter or the bylaws.

§ 230. Exception to requirements of notice.

Required notice [see § 229] need not be given to

(a) any person with whom communication is unlawful (if applicable, any certificate required to be filed under this chapter shall state that notice was not given to such persons);

(b) any stockholder/member if

(1) notice of 2 consecutive annual meetings, and any intervening notices of meetings or of actions by written consent, or

(2) all, and at least 2, payments (if sent by first-class mail) of dividends or interest on securities during a 12-month period,

mailed[14] to such person at her record address have been returned undeliverable (but such person can reinstate the notice requirement by delivering to the corporation a written notice of her then current address).

§ 231. Voting procedures and inspectors of elections.

(a) The corporation shall, in advance of any stockholder meeting, appoint 1 or more inspectors to act at the meeting and make a written report thereof. It may designate alternates. If no inspector or alternate is able to act at the meeting, the person presiding shall appoint 1 or more inspectors. Before assuming her duties, each inspector "shall take and sign an oath faithfully to execute the duties of inspector with strict impartiality and according to the best of such inspector's ability."

(b) "The inspectors shall:

(1) Ascertain the number of shares outstanding and the voting power of each;

(2) Determine the shares represented at a meeting and the validity of proxies and ballots;

---

[14] Subsection (c) clarifies that "mailed" does *not* include electronic submission.

Warning: The legal texts presented here have been altered. Do not rely on them for legal advice

(3) Count all votes and ballots;

(4) Determine and retain for a reasonable period a record of the disposition of any challenges made to any determination by the inspectors; and

(5) Certify their determination of the number of shares represented at the meeting, and their count of all votes and ballots.

The inspectors may appoint or retain other persons or entities to assist the inspectors in the performance of the duties of the inspectors."

(c) The polling hours for each matter shall be announced at the meeting. After the closing of the polls, no votes or changes thereto shall be accepted, unless the Court of Chancery upon application by a stockholder determines otherwise.

(d) "In determining the validity and counting of proxies and ballots, the inspectors shall be limited to an examination of the proxies, any envelopes submitted with those proxies, any information provided in accordance with [§§ 211(e), 212©(2), or 211(a)(2)(B)(i) or (iii)], ballots and the regular books and records of the corporation, except that the inspectors may consider other reliable information for the limited purpose of reconciling proxies and ballots submitted by or on behalf of banks, brokers, their nominees or similar persons which represent more votes than the holder of a proxy is authorized by the record owner to cast or more votes than the stockholder holds of record. If the inspectors consider other reliable information for the limited purpose permitted herein, the inspectors at the time they make their certification pursuant to subsection (b)(5) of this section shall specify the precise information considered by them including the person or persons from whom they obtained the information, when the information was obtained, the means by which the information was obtained and the basis for the inspectors' belief that such information is accurate and reliable."

(e) This section only applies to corporations having at least one class of voting stock

(1) listed on a national securities exchange;

(2) authorized for quotation on an interdealer quotation system of a registered national securities association; or

(3) held of record by more than 2,000 stockholders.

§ 232. Notice by electronic transmission.

(a) A form of electronic transmission suffices for required notice if the stockholder consented to this form. The stockholder can revoke the consent in writing. The consent lapses if (1) two consecutive notices of this form are undeliverable and (2) this becomes known to any person responsible for the giving of notice; but the inadvertent failure to recognize the lapse shall not invalidate any meeting or other action.

(b) Notice pursuant to subsection (a) is given, if by

    (1) facsimile (or (2) email): when directed to a number (email address) consented to by the stockholder;

    (3) a posting on an electronic network together with separate notice to the stockholder of such specific posting: upon the later of the two; and

    (4) any other form of electronic transmission: when directed to the stockholder.

    In the absence of fraud, an affidavit of electronic transmission of any agent of the corporation is prima facie evidence of the facts stated therein.

(c) "For purposes of this chapter, "electronic transmission" means any form of communication, not directly involving the physical transmission of paper, including the use of, or participation in, one or more electronic networks or databases (including one or more distributed electronic networks or databases), that creates a record that may be retained, retrieved and reviewed by a recipient thereof, and that may be directly reproduced in paper form by such a recipient through an automated process."

(d) [repealed]

(e) This section shall not apply to § 164, 296, 311, 312, or 324.

§ 233. Notice to stockholders sharing an address.

(a) A single written notice suffices for required notice if stockholders share an address and consented to this. The stockholders can revoke the consent in writing.

(b) If the corporation provides written notice of its intention to proceed under paragraph (a), failure to object in writing within 60 days constitutes consent.

(c) [repealed]

(d) This section shall not apply to § 164, 296, 311, 312 or 324.

SUBCHAPTER VIII. AMENDMENT OF CERTIFICATE OF INCORPORATION; CHANGES IN CAPITAL AND CAPITAL STOCK

§ 241. Amendment of certificate of incorporation before receipt of payment for stock.

Before a corporation has received any payment for any of its stock, or a nonstock corporation has any members:

(a)/(b)/(c) A majority of the directors (or of the incorporators, if the corporation does not have directors yet) may amend the bylaws by filing in accordance with § 103(a)-(d) a certificate setting forth the amendment and certifying the foregoing. The amendment is

- **permissible** so long as the amended charter would be lawful as an original charter at the time of the filing of the amendment, but
- **effective** as of the date on which the original charter became effective, except as to those persons who are substantially and adversely affected by the amendment.

§ 242. Amendment of certificate of incorporation after receipt of payment for stock; nonstock corporations.

After a corporation has received payment for any of its capital stock, or a nonstock corporation has members:

(a) **[Permissibility]** Amendments are permissible if the amended charter would be lawful as an original charter at the time of the filing of the amendment. The amended charter may contain transitional provisions necessary to effect any change.

(b) **[Procedure]** Amendments require:

(1) **[stock corporation]** If the corporation has capital stock:

- A **board resolution** setting forth the amendment, declaring its advisability, and either calling a special stockholder meeting or directing that the amendment be considered at the next annual meeting (the stockholder meeting notice shall set forth the full amendment or a brief summary, unless it constitutes a notice of internet availability of proxy materials under the SEC rules);

- The affirmative vote of a **majority of the outstanding stock,** and of a majority of each class entitled to a class vote;[15] and
- **Filing** of an amendment certificate in accordance with §103(a)-(d).

(2) **[class vote in stock corporation]** A class vote is required if the amendment would change

- the par value of shares of such class;
- the aggregate number of authorized shares of such class (unless, for shares not outstanding, the current charter provides otherwise); or
- "the powers, preferences, or special rights of the shares of such class so as to affect them adversely" (but if the change so affects only some of the series of such class, then only these series get a class vote). *↳ must directly impacted to get a vote*

(3) **[nonstock corporation]** If the corporation is a nonstock corporation:

- A resolution of the governing body approved by a majority of all its members and setting forth the amendment and declaring its advisability; and
- Filing of an amendment certificate in accordance with §103(a)-(d).
- The charter may additionally require approval by a specified number or percentage of members or a class of members.

(4) **[supermajority provisions]** If a charter provision requires for some action a greater number or proportion of votes than is required by this title, such provision shall not be amended except by such greater vote.

(c) **[board abandonment reservation]** The resolution authorizing the amendment may provide that the board or governing body may abandon

---

[15] No stockholder vote is required to change the corporate name; or to delete provisions of the original charter naming incorporators, the initial board, and the original subscribers, or transitional provisions in an amended charter for changes that have become effective. *not impacting Sth rights or relationship*

Warning: The legal texts presented here have been altered. Do not rely on them for legal advice

such amendment at any time prior to the effectiveness of the filing of the certificate.

§ 243. Retirement of stock.

(a) The board may retire shares issued but not outstanding.

(b) Retired shares become authorized and unissued. To the extent the charter prohibits reissuance, a certificate stating this and the shares' retirement shall be filed in accordance with § 103(a)-(d). Such certificate amends the charter so as to reduce accordingly the number of authorized shares and, where applicable, removing all references to a retired class.

(c) A reduction of capital in connection with the retirement is subject to § 244.

§ 244. Reduction of capital.

(a) **[Procedure]** The board may reduce the corporation's capital:

(1) By reducing the capital represented by retired shares;

(2)/(3) By applying to an otherwise authorized purchase, redemption, conversion, or exchange of outstanding shares, capital represented by such shares or any capital that has not been allocated to any particular class (to the extent that such capital exceeds the total par value or the stated capital of shares issuable upon such conversion or exchange, if any); or

(4) By transferring to surplus (i) capital not represented by any particular class; (ii) capital represented by, but in excess of the aggregate par value of, issued par stock; or (iii) some but not all of the capital represented by issued no-par stock.

(b) **[solvency condition; shareholder liability]** The corporation's remaining assets must be sufficient to pay any of its debts for which payment has not been otherwise provided. "No reduction of capital shall release any liability of any stockholder whose shares have not been fully paid."

§ 245. Restated certificate of incorporation.

(a) A corporation may, whenever desired, integrate into a single instrument ("restated charter") all of the provisions of its charter.

(b) If the restated charter merely restates and integrates but does not further amend the charter, it may be adopted by the board without a stockholder vote, or pursuant to the amendment procedure of § 242.

(b)/(e) If the restated charter does further amend the charter, it must be adopted pursuant to the amendment procedure of § 242 or 241, as applicable, and comply with this chapter's other rules for amendments.

(c) A restated charter shall be specifically designated as such in its heading. It shall state, either in its heading or in an introductory paragraph, the corporation's present and original name(s), and the filing date of its original charter. A restated charter shall also state that it was duly adopted in accordance with this section. A restated charter may omit (a) provisions of the original charter which named the incorporators, the initial board and the original subscribers, and (b) provisions contained in any charter amendment as were necessary to effect a change now effective. Such omissions are not a further amendment.

(d) A restated charter shall be executed, acknowledged and filed in accordance with § 103. Once filed, the amended charter supersedes the prior charter, but the original date of incorporation remains unchanged.

§ 246. [Reserved.]

SUBCHAPTER IX. MERGER, CONSOLIDATION OR CONVERSION

§ 251. Merger or consolidation of domestic corporations.

(a) **[principle] Corporations may merge** into a single surviving corporation (which may be either of the constituent corporations) or consolidate into a new resulting corporation formed by the consolidation, **pursuant to an agreement of merger or consolidation** ("the agreement").

(b) **[board resolution]** The board of each corporation shall adopt a resolution approving the agreement and declaring its advisability. The agreement shall state:

(1) The terms and conditions of the merger or consolidation;

(2) the mode of carrying the same into effect;

(3) in the case of a merger, any amendments or changes in the charter of the surviving corporation;

(4) in the case of a consolidation, the charter of the resulting corporation;

---

(5) the manner, if any, of converting the shares of each of the constituent corporations into cash, property, and/or shares or other securities of the surviving or resulting (hereinafter generically "surviving") or any other corporation; and

(6) such other details or provisions as are deemed desirable.

The agreement shall be executed and acknowledged in accordance with § 103. Any of its terms may be conditioned upon facts ascertainable outside of such agreement, provided that the manner in which the condition will operate is clearly and expressly set forth in the agreement.

(c-1) **[shareholder vote]** The executed agreement shall be approved by a majority of the outstanding voting rights of each corporation at an annual or special meeting. Due notice of the time, place and purpose of the meeting shall be mailed to each holder of stock, whether voting or nonvoting, at the stockholder's record address, at least 20 days prior to the date of the meeting; the notice shall contain a copy of the agreement or a brief summary thereof.

(c-2) **[filing; effectiveness]** The agreement shall then be filed, and shall become effective, in accordance with § 103. The secretary or assistant secretary of the corporation shall certify stockholder approval [or adoption pursuant to, and satisfaction of the conditions of, subsections (f), (g), or (h)] on the agreement to be filed.

In lieu of certifying and filing the agreement, the surviving corporation may file a certificate of merger or consolidation ("the certificate"), executed in accordance with § 103, which states all of the above and that the executed agreement is on file at an office of the surviving corporation (stating its address) and that a copy will be furnished, on request and without cost, to any stockholder of any constituent corporation.

[In the cases of subsections (f), (g), or (h), such filing constitutes a representation by the person who executes the agreement that the facts stated in the certificate remain true immediately prior to such filing.]

(d) The agreement may provide that until it becomes effective in accordance with § 103, it may be terminated by the board of any constituent corporation, or, subject to the conditions listed below, amended by the boards of the constituent corporations; if such termination/amendment occurs after the filing of the agreement/certificate with the Secretary of

Warning: The legal texts presented here have been altered. Do not rely on them for legal advice

66

State, a certificate of termination/amendment shall be filed in accordance with § 103. Such an amendment shall not change (1) the merger consideration to be received by stockholders, (2) the charter of the surviving corporation, or (3) any of the terms and conditions of the agreement if such change would adversely affect the holders of any class or series of stock.

(e) **[charter amendment]** In the case of a merger, the charter of the surviving corporation shall automatically be amended to the extent, if any, that changes in the charter are set forth in the agreement.

(f) **[≤20% stock issued]** In the case of a merger, no vote of the stockholders of the surviving corporation is necessary if the surviving corporation's charter and outstanding stock remain unaffected and no more than 20% of its common stock outstanding immediately prior to the merger is to be issued (or, in the case of treasury shares, delivered) under the plan of merger. A stockholder vote is also unnecessary if the corporation does not have any stock outstanding.

(g) **[holding company reorganization]** In the case of a merger, no vote of the stockholders of the corporation is necessary to authorize a merger with a direct or indirect wholly-owned Delaware subsidiary (corporation or LLC) if:

    (5) as a result of the merger the corporation or its successor becomes or remains a direct or indirect wholly-owned subsidiary of a Delaware holding company (as defined below);

    (1) the corporation and its subsidiary are the only participants in the merger,

    (2) each share of capital stock of the corporation is converted in the merger into a share of holding company capital stock having the same rights;

    (4)/(6) the charter, by-laws, and directors of the *holding company* will be the same as those of the corporation;

    (7) the organizational documents (charter or limited liability company agreement, as the case may be) of the *surviving entity* contain provisions identical to the charter of the corporation, provided that:

        (i) they must also contain

    (A)/(B) a requirement that holding company stockholders approve any act other than the election or removal of directors or managers that requires (or would require, if the surviving entity were an LLC) the approval of the stockholders of the surviving entity under its charter or this chapter;

    (C) if the surviving entity is an LLC, a provision that the LLC be managed by or under the direction of a governing body consisting of individuals who are subject to the same fiduciary duties applicable to, and who are liable for breach of such duties to the same extent as, directors of a corporation

    (ii) the merger may (A) reduce the number of authorized classes and shares of equity interests, and (B) eliminate any provision authorized by §141(d), and

(8) the stockholders of the corporation do not recognize gain or loss for US federal income tax purposes as determined by the board of directors of the constituent corporation.

A "holding company" is a Delaware corporation which, from its incorporation until consummation of a merger governed by this subsection, was at all times a direct or indirect wholly-owned subsidiary of the corporation and whose capital stock is issued in such merger.

The restrictions of § 203 shall remain unaffected by such holding company merger, i.e., they shall, with respect to timing, interested person status, and so on, apply to the holding company's stock and stockholders as if they were the corporation's stock and its stockholders. If the corporate name of the holding company immediately following the effective time of the merger is the name of the corporation immediately prior, the stock certificates that previously represented shares of capital stock of the corporation shall now represent the shares of capital stock of the holding company into which they were converted. To the extent a stockholder of the corporation immediately prior to the merger had standing to institute or maintain derivative litigation on behalf of the corporation, he maintains such standing.

(h) **[back-end squeeze-out]** No vote of stockholders of a constituent corporation ("the target") that has a class or series of shares listed on a national securities exchange or held of record by more than 2,000 holders immediately prior to the execution of the merger agreement shall be necessary to authorize a merger if:

(1) the agreement expressly

    a. permits or requires such merger to be effected under this subsection; and

    b. provides that the merger, if effected under this subsection, shall be effected as soon as practicable following the consummation of the offer referred to in paragraph (2);

(2)/(4) on the terms provided in the agreement, the other constituent corporation ("the offeror") Consummates an offer for all of the ✓ target's stock that would be entitled to vote on the merger absent this subsection (the offer may contain minimum tender conditions, be separated by class or series of stock, and exclude Excluded Stock);

(3) immediately following the offer's Consummation, the stock owned by the offeror and its Affiliates, including Rollover Stock and stock irrevocably accepted for purchase pursuant to the offer and Received by the Depository, constitute at least such percentage of each class or series of the target's stock that, absent this subsection, would be required to adopt the agreement; and

(5) the merger consideration for target shares (excluding Excluded Stock) is the same as the offer consideration.

(6) As used in this section only, the term:

    a. "Affiliate" means (i) any person that owns, directly or indirectly, all of the outstanding stock of the offeror, and (ii) such person's direct or indirect wholly-owned subsidiaries.

    b. "Consummate" means irrevocably accept for purchase or exchange stock tendered pursuant to an offer;

    c. "Depository" means an agent appointed to facilitate consummation of the offer;

    d. "Excluded Stock" is (i) stock owned at the commencement of the offer by the offeror, the offeror's Affiliates, the target, or the target's wholly-owned subsidiaries, and (ii) Rollover Stock.

e. "Person" means any individual, corporation, partnership, limited liability company, unincorporated association or other entity;

f. "Received" means "(a) with respect to certificated shares, physical receipt of a stock certificate accompanied by an executed letter of transmittal, (b) with respect to uncertificated shares held of record by a clearing corporation as nominee, transfer into the depository's account by means of an agent's message, and (c) with respect to uncertificated shares held of record by a person other than a clearing corporation as nominee, physical receipt of an executed letter of transmittal by the depository; provided, however, that shares shall cease to be "received" (i) with respect to certificated shares, if the certificate representing such shares was canceled prior to consummation of the offer referred to in paragraph (h)(2) of this section, or (ii) with respect to uncertificated shares, to the extent such uncertificated shares have been reduced or eliminated due to any sale of such shares prior to consummation of the offer referred to in paragraph (h)(2) of this section;" and

g. "Rollover Stock" are target shares subject of a written agreement requiring such shares to be transferred, contributed or delivered to the offeror or any of its Affiliates in exchange for equity interests in the offeror or any of its Affiliates; so long as such shares are in fact so transferred, contributed or delivered prior to the effective time of the merger.

§ 252. Merger or consolidation of domestic and foreign corporations; service of process upon surviving or resulting corporation.

(a) Mergers or consolidations are also possible with corporations of another jurisdiction (state or country) if that jurisdiction's law so permits.

(b) All the constituent corporations shall enter into an agreement of merger or consolidation. The agreement shall contain all the provisions required in domestic mergers pursuant to § 251(b), provided, however, that the laws of the jurisdiction chosen to govern the surviving or resulting corporation determine what can or must be included regarding the terms of its charter.

(c) "The agreement shall be adopted, approved, certified, executed and acknowledged by each of the constituent corporations in accordance with the laws under which it is organized, and, in the case of a [Delaware corporation], in the same manner as is provided in § 251" and including the possibility to file certificate of merger or consolidation in lieu of filing the agreement.

(d) If the surviving corporation is a foreign corporation, it shall agree that it may be served with process in Delaware in any proceeding for enforcement of any obligation of any constituent Delaware corporation, as well as for enforcement of any obligation of the surviving corporation arising from the merger or consolidation, including any suit to enforce appraisal rights under § 262, and shall irrevocably appoint the Secretary of State as its agent to accept service of process in any such suit and shall specify the address to which a copy of such process shall be mailed by the Secretary of State. The Secretary of State is authorized to issue such rules with respect to such service as the Secretary deems appropriate. The Secretary of State must forthwith forward a copy of any process so served to the surviving corporation. ...

(e) §251(d) applies to any merger or consolidation under this section; subsection §251(e) applies to a merger under this section in which the surviving corporation is a corporation of this State; and § 251(f) and (h) apply to any merger under this section.

§ 253. Merger of parent corporation and subsidiary corporation or corporations.

(a) If (1) one corporation's ("the parent") ownership in another corporation[16] or corporations ("the subsidiary") amounts to at least 90% of the outstanding shares of each class of stock entitled to vote on a merger and (2) at least one of these corporations is a Delaware corporation and unless the laws of a foreign corporation prohibit such merger, the parent may merge into or with the subsidiary simply by executing, acknowledging and filing, in accordance with § 103, a certificate of such ownership and merger setting forth a copy of the resolution of its board to so merge and the date of the adoption ("short-form merger").

---

[16] Other than a surviving entity in a DGCL 251(g) transaction.

Warning: The legal texts presented here have been altered. Do not rely on them for legal advice

If the parent owns less than 100% of the subsidiary, the resolution of the parent's board shall state the terms and conditions of the merger, including the merger consideration paid to the subsidiary's minority shareholders. Conditions are allowed to the same extent as in a normal merger.

If the parent is not the surviving corporation, the resolution shall include provision for the pro rata issuance of stock of the surviving corporation to the holders of the stock of the parent corporation on surrender of any certificates therefor, and the certificate of ownership and merger shall state that the proposed merger has been approved by a majority of the outstanding stock of the parent entitled to vote thereon at a meeting duly called and held after 20 days' notice of the purpose of the meeting mailed to each such stockholder at the stockholder's record address (or the laws of the relevant foreign jurisdiction if the parent is a foreign corporation).

§§ 252(d) and 258(c) apply to short-form mergers.

(b) If the surviving corporation is a Delaware corporation, it may change its corporate name by the inclusion of a provision to that effect in the resolution of merger adopted by the directors of the parent and set forth in the certificate of ownership and merger.

(c) § 251(d) applies to a short-form merger, and § 251(e) applies to a short-form merger in which the surviving corporation is a Delaware subsidiary. References to "agreement of merger" in § 251(d), (e) shall mean for purposes of this subsection the resolution of merger adopted by the parent's board. A merger which effects any changes other than those authorized by this section or made applicable by this subsection cannot be accomplished as a short-form merger. **§ 262 shall not apply to short-form mergers, except as provided in subsection (d) of this section.**

(d) In the event of a short-form merger involving a Delaware subsidiary not 100% owned by the parent, the stockholders of the Delaware subsidiary shall have appraisal rights as set forth in § 262.

(e) This section applies to nonstock corporations if the surviving corporation is the nonstock parent corporation.

(f) This section does not authorize a merger with a charitable nonstock corporation if the charitable status is lost through the merger.

§§ 254-258: Mergers of Nonstock Corporations and Joint Stock Associations [OMITTED]

§ 259. Status, rights, liabilities, of constituent and surviving or resulting corporations following merger or consolidation

(a) Upon the effectiveness of the merger or consolidation, "the separate existence of all the constituent corporations .. shall cease," and the surviving or resulting corporation, as the case may be, shall have all the rights and obligations of the constituent corporations.

(b) In the case of a merger of banks or trust companies serving in a fiduciary capacity, any party in interest may apply to an appropriate court for a determination whether a new and different fiduciary should be appointed.

§ 260. Powers of corporation surviving or resulting from merger or consolidation; issuance of stock, bonds or other indebtedness

The surviving or resulting corporation may issue obligations to an amount sufficient with its capital stock to provide for all the payments or obligations necessary to effect the merger or consolidation. To secure the payment of such obligations, the surviving or resulting corporation may mortgage its assets. The surviving or resulting corporation may issue stock and other securities to the stockholders of the constituent corporations in exchange or payment for the original shares, in accordance with the terms of the agreement of merger or consolidation.

§ 261. Effect of merger upon pending actions

Any pending proceeding by or against any corporation party to a merger or consolidation shall be prosecuted as if the latter had not taken place, or the surviving or resulting corporation may be substituted in such proceeding.

§ 262. Appraisal rights.

(a) Any stockholder of record ("stockholder") of a Delaware corporation who holds shares of stock on the date of the making of a demand pursuant to subsection (d) with respect to such shares, who continuously holds such shares through the effective date of the merger or consolidation, and who has not voted in favor of the merger, shall be entitled to an appraisal by the Court of Chancery of the fair value of the stockholder's shares of stock subject to the conditions of subsections (b) through (d).

(b) Appraisal rights are available in a merger to be effected pursuant to §§ 251-258 (except §251(g)), 263-264, or 267, and in a conversion to a public benefit corporation pursuant to § 363(a).

   (1) However, ~~no~~ appraisal rights are available in a merger (except pursuant to §§ 253, 267, and 363(a)) for

   - **any stock** or depositary receipts in respect thereof ~~that~~, at the record date fixed for the merger vote (or, in the case of a merger pursuant to § 251(h), immediately prior to the execution of the merger agreement), were either **(i) listed on a national securities exchange** or (ii) **held of record by more than 2,000 holders,** and

   - any stock of the surviving corporation whose vote was not required to approve the merger pursuant to **§ 251(f),** …

   (2) … **if** the holders of such stock or depositary receipts **can receive** for their stock under the terms of the merger **shares** of stock (or corresponding depositary receipts) of either

      a. the surviving corporation or

      b. any other corporation, which stock at the effective date of the merger or consolidation will be either listed on a national securities exchange or held of record by more than 2,000 holders,

      and, where applicable, cash in lieu of fractional shares.

   (3) In a short-form merger under §§ 253 or 267 involving a Delaware subsidiary, appraisal rights are only available for the subsidiary's shareholders.

   (4) The procedures of this section for "mergers" apply as nearly as practicable to a conversion to a public benefit corporation by amendment pursuant to § 363(a)/(b).

(c) The charter may provide for appraisal rights in case of its amendment, any merger, or the sale of all or substantially all of the assets of the corporation. In this case, the provisions of this section shall apply as nearly as is practicable.

(d) Appraisal rights shall be perfected as follows:

(1) With respect to all shares for which appraisal rights are available under subsections (b) and (c), the corporation shall notify each holder of record of such rights not less than 20 days prior to the shareholder meeting set to vote on the merger, and shall include in such notice a copy of this section (and of §114, if one of the constituent corporations is a nonstock corporation). **To perfect his appraisal rights, a stockholder must deliver a separate written demand for appraisal to the corporation before the stockholder vote.** Within 10 days after the effective date of the merger, the surviving corporation shall notify each stockholder who has complied with this subsection and has not voted in favor of the merger of the date that the merger has become effective; or

(2) In a short-form merger under §§ 251(h), 253 or 267, or in a merger approved by written consent pursuant to § 228, it is sufficient if notice of the appraisal rights is given to eligible stockholders until within 10 days after the effective date of the merger. Within 20 days after the mailing date of such notice (or, in the case of §251(h), within the later of the consummation of the offer and 20 days after such mailing date) any eligible stockholder may demand in writing the appraisal from the surviving corporation.

In that same or a separate notice and within the same time-limit, the corporation or the surviving corporation must also inform all eligible stockholders of the effective date of the merger.

"An affidavit of the secretary or assistant secretary or of the transfer agent of the corporation that is required to give either notice that such notice has been given shall, in the absence of fraud, be prima facie evidence of the facts stated therein."

"For purposes of determining the stockholders entitled to receive either notice, each constituent corporation may fix, in advance, a record date that shall be not more than 10 days prior to the date the notice is given, provided, that if the notice is given on or after the effective date of the merger or consolidation, the record date shall be such effective date. If no record date is fixed and the notice is given prior to the effective date, the record date shall be the close of business on the day next preceding the day on which the notice is given."

(e) Within 120 days after the effective date of the merger, the surviving corporation or any stockholder who has complied with subsections (a) and (d) and who is otherwise entitled to appraisal rights, may file a petition in the Court of Chancery demanding a determination of the value of the stock of all such stockholders. However, within 60 days after the effective date of the merger, any stockholder who has not filed such petition or joined the proceeding as a named party can withdraw his demand for appraisal and accept the merger terms.

The surviving corporation shall mail a written notice of the aggregate number of shares and shareholders who did not vote in favor of the merger and demanded appraisal (or, in the case of § 251(h), were not tendered, other than any excluded stock as defined in § 251(h)(6)d.) to any shareholder who so requests within 120 days after the effective date of the merger and who has complied with the requirements of subsections (a) and (d), within 10 days after the later of (1) receipt of the shareholder's written request and (2) expiration of the period for delivery of demands for appraisal under subsection (d).

Notwithstanding subsection (a), beneficial owners of stock held in street name can in their own name file the petition and make the request described in this subsection.

(f) The **petition**, if filed by the surviving corporation, shall be accompanied by a duly verified list containing the names and addresses of all stockholders who have demanded payment for their shares and with whom agreements as to the value of their shares have not been reached. If the petition is filed by a stockholder, service of a copy thereof shall be made upon the surviving corporation, which shall file such duly verified list within 20 days after such service in the office of the Register in Chancery.

"The Register in Chancery, if so ordered by the Court, shall give notice of the time and place fixed for the hearing of such petition by registered or certified mail to the surviving corporation and to the stockholders shown on the list at the addresses therein stated. Such notice shall also be given by 1 or more publications at least 1 week before the day of the hearing, in a newspaper of general circulation published in the City of Wilmington, Delaware or such publication as the Court deems advisable. The forms of the notices by mail and by publication shall be approved by the Court, and the costs thereof shall be borne by the surviving corporation."

At the hearing on such petition, the Court shall, ...

(g) **... first, determine the stockholders who have complied with this section and who have become entitled to appraisal rights.** However, the Court may proceed to trial upon the appraisal prior to the final determination, and until such final determination any stockholder named on the list filed by the surviving corporation pursuant to subsection (f) may participate fully in all proceedings.

"The Court may require the stockholders who have demanded an appraisal for their shares and who hold stock represented by certificates to submit their certificates of stock to the Register in Chancery for notation thereon of the pendency of the appraisal proceedings; and if any stockholder fails to comply with such direction, the Court may dismiss the proceedings as to such stockholder."

The Court shall dismiss the proceedings with respect to shares listed on a national securities exchange immediately before the merger unless (1) the total number of shares entitled to appraisal exceeds 1% of the outstanding shares of their class or series, (2) the merger consideration for such total number of shares exceeds $1 million, or (3) the merger was approved pursuant to § 253 or § 267.

(h) **... second, appraise the shares, determining the shares' fair value "exclusive of any element of value arising from the accomplishment or expectation of the merger."** In so doing, the Court may consider all relevant factors. Interest shall be paid from the effective date of the merger through the date of payment. Unless the Court of Chancery determines otherwise in its discretion for good cause shown, interest shall be compounded quarterly and shall accrue at 5% over the Federal Reserve discount rate (including any surcharge). If at any time before the entry of judgment, the surviving corporation pays to each stockholder entitled to appraisal an amount in cash, interest shall accrue thereafter only upon the difference, if any, between the amount so paid, and the fair value of the shares as determined by the Court plus interest theretofore accrued. The Court may, in its discretion, proceed with this step (h) before concluding step (g).

Warning: The legal texts presented here have been altered. Do not rely on them for legal advice

(i) **... third, direct the payment of the appraised amount to the stockholders entitled thereto.** In the case of shares represented by certificates, payment shall be conditioned upon the surrender to the corporation of the certificates.

(j) "The costs of the proceeding may be determined by the Court and taxed upon the parties as the Court deems equitable in the circumstances.

Upon application of a stockholder, the Court may order all or a portion of the **expenses incurred by any stockholder in connection with the appraisal** proceeding, including, without limitation, reasonable attorney's fees and the fees and expenses of experts, **to be charged pro rata** against the value of all the shares entitled to an appraisal."

(k) From the effective date of the merger, no stockholder who has demanded appraisal rights as provided in subsection (d) shall be entitled to vote such stock for any purpose or to receive payment of dividends or other distributions on the stock (except dividends or other distributions payable to stockholders of record at a date which is prior to the effective date of the merger); provided, however, that if no petition for an appraisal shall be filed within the time provided in subsection (e), or if such stockholder shall deliver to the surviving corporation a written withdrawal of such stockholder's demand for an appraisal and an acceptance of the merger or consolidation, either within 60 days after the effective date of the merger as provided in subsection (e) or thereafter with the written approval of the corporation, then the right of such stockholder to an appraisal shall cease.

Notwithstanding the foregoing, no appraisal proceeding in the Court of Chancery shall be dismissed as to any stockholder without the approval of the Court, and such approval may be conditioned upon such terms as the Court deems just.

(l) The shares of the surviving corporation to which the shares of such objecting stockholders would have been converted had they assented to the merger shall have the status of authorized and unissued shares of the surviving corporation.

[§ 263 et seq. OMITTED]

Guide to the Federal Proxy Rules

17 C.F.R. 240

§240.14a-1 et seq.: Regulation 14A: Solicitation of Proxies

14a-1 Definitions. [verbatim]

Unless the context otherwise requires, all terms used in this regulation have the same meanings as in the Act or elsewhere in the general rules and regulations thereunder. In addition, the following definitions apply unless the context otherwise requires:

...

(f) Proxy. The term "proxy" includes every proxy, consent or authorization within the meaning of section 14(a) of the Act. The consent or authorization may take the form of failure to object or to dissent.

(g) Proxy statement. The term "proxy statement" means the statement required by rule 14a 3(a) whether or not contained in a single document.

...

(j) Registrant. The term "registrant" means the issuer of the securities in respect of which proxies are to be solicited.

...

(l) Solicitation.

    (1) The terms "solicit" and "solicitation" include:

        (i) Any request for a proxy whether or not accompanied by or included in a form of proxy;

        (ii) Any request to execute or not to execute, or to revoke, a proxy; or

---

(iii) The furnishing of a form of proxy or other communication to security holders under circumstances reasonably calculated to result in the procurement, withholding or revocation of a proxy.

(2) The terms do not apply, however, to:

(i) The furnishing of a form of proxy to a security holder upon the unsolicited request of such security holder;

(ii) The performance by the registrant of acts required by rule 14a–7;

(iii) The performance by any person of ministerial acts on behalf of a person soliciting a proxy; or

(iv) **A communication** by a security holder who does not otherwise engage in a proxy solicitation (other than a solicitation exempt under rule 14a–2) **stating how the security holder intends to vote** and the reasons therefor, provided that the communication:

(A) Is made by means of **speeches in public forums, press releases**, published or broadcast opinions, statements, or **advertisements** appearing in a broadcast media, or newspaper, magazine or other bona fide publication disseminated on a regular basis,

(B) Is directed to persons to whom the security holder owes a fiduciary duty in connection with the voting of securities of a registrant held by the security holder, or

(C) Is made in response to unsolicited requests for additional information with respect to a prior communication by the security holder made pursuant to this paragraph (l)(2)(iv).

14a-2 Solicitations to which Rules 14a–3 to 14a–15 apply.

Rules 14a–3 to 14a–15 apply to **every proxy solicitation** with respect to registered securities, **except**:

(a)

(1) [forwarding of proxy materials by brokers];

(2) [solicitation by beneficial owner (from broker etc.)];

(3) - (5) …

(6) "Any solicitation through the medium of a newspaper advertisement which informs security holders of a source from which they may obtain copies of a proxy statement, form of proxy and any other soliciting material and does no more than:

(i) Name the registrant,

(ii) State the reason for the advertisement, and

(iii) Identify the proposal or proposals to be acted upon by security holders."

(b) The following, which are, however, subject to 14a-6(g), 14a-7, and 14a-9:

(1) Any solicitation by any person who **does not seek**, either on its own or another's behalf, **the power to act as proxy** and does not furnish or otherwise request a form of revocation, abstention, consent or authorization. **Exceptions**: This exemption shall not apply to:

(i) The **registrant**;

(ii) "An **officer or director of the registrant** or any person serving in a similar capacity engaging in a solicitation **financed directly or indirectly by the registrant**;"

(iii) ...;

(iv) "Any **nominee** for whose election as a director proxies are solicited;"

(v) "Any person soliciting in **opposition to a merger**, recapitalization, reorganization, sale of assets or other extraordinary transaction recommended or approved by the board of directors of the registrant who is **proposing** or intends to propose **an alternative transaction** to which such person or one of its affiliates is a party;"

(vi) "Any person who is required to report beneficial ownership of the registrant's equity securities on a **Schedule 13D**, unless such person has filed a Schedule 13D and has not disclosed pursuant to Item 4 thereto an intent, or reserved the right, to engage in a control transaction, or any contested solicitation for the election of directors;"

(vii) – (viii) ...;

(ix) "Any person who, because of a substantial interest in the subject matter of the solicitation, is likely to receive a **benefit** from a successful solicitation that would **not** be **shared pro rata** by all other holders of the same class of securities, other than a benefit arising from the person's employment with the registrant; and"

(x) "Any person acting on behalf of any of the foregoing."

(2) "Any solicitation made otherwise than on behalf of the registrant where the **total number of persons solicited is not more than ten;**"

(3) [proxy advisory services];

(4) …;

(5) [research reports];

(6) [for solicitations in electronic shareholder forums up to 60 days before the meeting date, the exceptions for registrants etc. to paragraph (1) above do not apply];

(7)/(8) [relate to the so-called proxy access rule 14a-11, which was vacated by Business Roundtable v. SEC (D.C. Circuit 2011).]

14a-3   Information to be furnished to security holders.

(a) Each person solicited must (have) be(en) furnished with:

(1)/(3) A **publicly-filed preliminary or definitive proxy statement** containing the information specified in **Schedule 14A**. The solicitation must be in the form and manner described in **rule 14a– 16 unless** it …

(i) … relates to a business combination transaction.[1]

(ii) … may not do so under the laws of the registrant's state of incorporation.

(2) [or Form S–4, F–4, or N–14]

(b) If the solicitation is made on behalf of the registrant and relates to an annual meeting (or special meeting or written consent in lieu of such

---

[1] "Business combination transaction" is an exchange offer or any transaction specified in rule 145(1) under the 1933 Act, as well as transactions for cash consideration requiring disclosure under Item 14 of Schedule 14A.

Warning: The legal texts presented here have been altered. Do not rely on them for legal advice

meeting) at which **directors are to be elected**, each proxy statement shall be accompanied or preceded by an **annual report**, which contains:

(1) consolidated **balance sheets** for the two most recent fiscal years and **income statements** for the three most recent fiscal years prepared in accordance with Regulation S–X. Schedules or exhibits may be omitted. The financial statements must be **audited** unless filings of the statements with the SEC are also exempt from the audit requirement.

(2) They must comply with the legibility requirements of rule 14a-5(d).

Items required by **Regulation S-K**:

(3) supplementary financial information (Item 302).

(4) "**changes in and disagreements with accountants** on accounting and financial disclosure" (Item 304)

(5) (i) selected financial data (Item 301).

　　(ii) … "management's discussion and analysis of financial condition and results of operations" (Item 303)

　　(iii) **disclosures about market risk** (Item 305)

(7) **industry segments, classes of similar products or services, foreign and domestic operations and exports sales** (paragraphs (b), (c)(1)(i) and (d) of Item 101)

(9) stock price, dividends, and a performance graph (Items 201(a), (b), (c), and (e))

(6) a **brief description of the registrant's business** during the most recent fiscal year which will, in the opinion of management, indicate the general nature and scope of the registrant's business.

(8) the registrant's **directors and officers**, indicating their principal occupation employer.

(10) "an **undertaking** in … reasonably prominent type **to provide without charge** to each person solicited upon … written request … a copy of the registrant's annual report on **Form 10–K**, including the financial statements and the financial statement schedules …"

---

(11) "Subject to the foregoing requirements, the report may be in any form deemed suitable by management …"

"Note: Registrants are encouraged to utilize tables, schedules, charts and graphic illustrations of present financial information in an understandable manner. Any presentation of financial information must be consistent with the data in the financial statements contained in the report and, if appropriate, should refer to relevant portions of the financial statements and notes thereto."

(12) [Reserved]

(13) This paragraph (b) shall not apply, however, to solicitations before the financial statements are available if a solicitation is being made at the same time in opposition to the registrant and if the registrant's proxy statement includes an undertaking in bold face type to furnish such annual report to security holders to all persons being solicited at least 20 calendar days before the vote takes place or the written consent becomes effective.

(c) "Seven copies of the report sent to security holders pursuant to this rule shall be mailed to the Commission ..."

(d) "An annual report to security holders prepared on an integrated basis pursuant to General Instruction H to Form 10–K may also be submitted in satisfaction of this section. ..."

(e) (1) [delivery to security holders with shared address]; (2) [no obligation to send if twice undeliverable]

(f) "The provisions of **paragraph (a)** of this section **shall not apply to a communication made by means of** speeches in public forums, press releases, published or broadcast opinions, statements, or advertisements appearing in a broadcast media, newspaper, magazine or other **bona fide publication disseminated on a regular basis**, provided that:

(1) No form of proxy, consent or authorization or means to execute the same is provided to a security holder in connection with the communication; and

(2) At the time the communication is made, a definitive proxy statement is on file with the Commission pursuant to rule 14a–6(b)."

14a-4 Requirements as to proxy.

(a) "The form of proxy

> (1) "shall indicate in bold-face type ... on whose behalf the solicitation is made;

> (2) "Shall provide a specifically designated blank space for dating the proxy card; and

> (3) "Shall identify clearly and impartially each separate matter intended to be acted upon, ... No reference need be made, however, to proposals as to which discretionary authority is conferred pursuant to paragraph (c)."

(b)

> (1) The proxy form shall provide <u>tick-the-box choices</u> of approval, disapproval, or abstention for each separate matter other than elections and votes on the frequency of say-on-pay votes. To the extent the security holder does not specify a choice, a proxy may confer discretionary authority if the form of proxy states in bold-face type how it intends to vote the shares in such case.

> (2) A proxy form that provides for the **election of directors** shall set forth the names of persons nominated for election as directors, including any. Such proxy form must provide simple means and clear instructions to withhold authority for individual nominees, such as ballot boxes, strike-out, or blank spaces. Unless the proxy form includes shareholder nominees, it may also provide a means to grant or withhold authority for the nominees as a group; in that case, the proxy form may also provide, in bold-face type, that failure to indicate a choice will be interpreted as a grant of authority.

> *"Instructions. 1. Paragraph (2) does not apply in the case of a merger, consolidation or other plan if the election of directors is an integral part of the plan.*

> *2. If applicable state law gives legal effect to votes cast against a nominee, then in lieu of, or in addition to, providing a means for security holders to withhold authority to vote, the registrant should provide a similar means for security holders to vote against each nominee."*

Warning: The legal texts presented here have been altered. Do not rely on them for legal advice

(3) A proxy form that provides for a vote on the **frequency of say-on-pay votes** required by section 14A(a)(2) of the 1934 Act shall provide tick-the-box choices of 1, 2 or 3 years, or abstention.

(c) A proxy may confer **discretionary authority** for:

(3) **"matters which the persons making the solicitation do not know, a reasonable time before the solicitation, are to be presented at the meeting,** if a specific statement to that effect is made in the proxy statement or form of proxy."

If the solicitation is **by the registrant for an annual meeting**, however, the proxy can confer discretionary authority only if the registrant

(1) did not have notice of the matter at least 45 days before the date on which the registrant first sent its proxy materials for the prior year's annual meeting (provided this date is within 30 days of this year's) or a date specified by an advance notice provision, or

(2) includes, in the proxy statement, advice on the nature of the matter and how the registrant intends to exercise its discretion, and the proponent does not (i) within the time-frame of paragraph (1) provide a written statement of its intention to solicit at least the requisite majority of voting shares, (ii) include the same statement in its proxy materials filed under rule 14a–6, and (iii) immediately after soliciting this majority, provide a statement from any person with knowledge that the necessary steps have been taken to do so.

(4) "Approval of the minutes of the prior meeting if such approval does not amount to ratification of the action taken at that meeting;"

(5) "The election of any person to any office for which a bona fide nominee is named in the proxy statement and such nominee is unable to serve or for good cause will not serve."

(6) Any proposal omitted from the proxy statement and form pursuant to rules 14a–8 or 14a–9.

(7) Matters incident to the conduct of the meeting.

(d) **No proxy shall confer authority for**

(1) any election for which a bona fide nominee is not named in the proxy statement,

(2) any annual meeting other than the next,

(3) more than one meeting (including adjournments) or consent solicitation, or

(4) any action other than the action proposed to be taken in the proxy statement, or matters referred to in paragraph (c).

A person is not a **bona fide nominee**, and shall not be named as such, unless the person has consented to being named in the proxy statement and to serve if elected.

Nothing in this section 14a–4 shall prevent any person soliciting in support of a **minority slate** from seeking authority to vote for nominees named in the registrant's proxy statement, "so long as the soliciting party:

(i) Seeks authority to vote in the aggregate for the number of director positions then subject to election;

(ii) Represents that it will vote for all the registrant nominees, other than those registrant nominees specified by the soliciting party;

(iii) Provides the security holder an opportunity to withhold authority with respect to any other registrant nominee by writing the name of that nominee on the form of proxy; and

(iv) States on the form of proxy and in the proxy statement that there is no assurance that the registrant's nominees will serve if elected with any of the soliciting party's nominees."

(e) The proxy statement or form of proxy shall provide, subject to reasonable specified conditions, that **the proxy will be exercised**, in accordance with the choices indicated pursuant to paragraph (b).

(f) Before or with the proxy form, the security holder must receive a definitive proxy statement filed with the Commission pursuant to rule 14a–6(b).

14a-5   Presentation of information in proxy statement.

(a) Information shall be clearly presented (using tables where appropriate, and not necessarily in the order of the schedule), divided according to subject matter, and preceded by appropriate headings. Amounts should be in figures.

(b) Information that must be determined in the future may be stated in terms of present knowledge and intention. Information not reasonably available to the soliciting person may be omitted, if a brief statement of the reasons is given. Authority concerning each such matter shall not extend further than reasonably necessary.

(c) Information contained in any other proxy soliciting material may be incorporated by reference.

(d)

(1) "All printed proxy statements shall be in roman type at least as large and as legible as 10-point modern type, except that to the extent necessary for convenient presentation financial statements and other tabular data, but not the notes thereto, may be in roman type at least as large and as legible as 8-point modern type. All such type shall be leaded at least 2 points."

(2) "Where a proxy statement is delivered [electronically], issuers may satisfy legibility requirements ... by presenting all required information in a format readily communicated to investors."

(e) All proxy statements shall disclose, under an appropriate caption, the deadlines for inclusion into the registrant's proxy statement for the next annual meeting of (1) shareholder proposals under rule 14a-8, (2) shareholder proposals outside rule 14a-8, and (3) shareholder nominees to be included under applicable state or foreign law or the registrant's charter or bylaws.

(f) "If the date of the next annual meeting is subsequently advanced or delayed by more than 30 calendar days from the date of the annual meeting to which the proxy statement relates, the registrant shall, in a timely manner, inform shareholders of such change, and the new dates referred to in paragraphs (e)(1) and (e)(2) ..., by including a notice, under Item 5, in its earliest possible quarterly report on Form 10–Q ... or, if impracticable, any means reasonably calculated to inform shareholders."

14a-6   Filing requirements.

(a) **Preliminary proxy statement**. A preliminary proxy statement and form must be filed with the Commission at least 10 calendar days before they are first sent to security holders, or such shorter period as the Commission may authorize. A registrant shall not file preliminary materials, however, if the solicitation is uncontested, relates to an annual meeting or special meeting in lieu thereof, and the only matters to be acted upon are:

(1) "The election of directors"

   (4) including shareholder nominees;

(2) "The election, approval or ratification of accountant(s);"

(3) Shareholder proposals under rule 14a–8;

(5) Executive compensation plan as defined in Item 402(a)(b)(ii) of Regulation S–K; … and/or

(8) Say-on-pay votes pursuant to rule 14a–21(a), votes to determine the frequency of such say-on-pay votes pursuant to rule 14a–21(b), or any other shareholder advisory vote on executive compensation.

A registrant's solicitation is uncontested if the registrant in its proxy material does not comment upon or refer to a solicitation in opposition.

Note 1: "The filing of revised material does not recommence the ten day time period unless the revised material contains material revisions or material new proposal(s) that constitute a fundamental change in the proxy material."

Note 2: "The official responsible for the preparation of the proxy material should make every effort to verify the accuracy and completeness of the information required by the applicable rules. The preliminary material should be filed with the Commission at the earliest practicable date."

Note 3: A 'solicitation in opposition' includes: (a) Any solicitation opposing a proposal supported by the registrant; and (b) any solicitation supporting a proposal that the registrant does not expressly support, other than a shareholder proposal included in the registrant's proxy material pursuant to Rule 14a–8. The mere

---

inclusion in the registrant's proxy materials of a shareholder proposal under rule 14a-8 or of a shareholder nominee under applicable state or foreign law or the registrant's charter or bylaws does not constitute a "solicitation in opposition" even if the registrant opposes this proposal or nominee and solicits against it.

Note 4: If the preliminary materials are filed only because the solicitation is contested, this should be indicated in the transmittal letter to the Commission.

(b) **Definitive proxy statement** and other soliciting material. No later than the date they are first sent to security holders, copies of the definitive proxy statement, form, and all other soliciting materials must be filed with the Commission and any national securities exchange where the registrant has listed securities.

(c) Personal solicitation materials. In the case of personal solicitation, all written instructions or other materials discussing the merits and furnished to persons making the actual solicitation, must be filed with the Commission no later than the date the materials are first sent to these persons.

(d) Release dates. All filings pursuant to paragraphs (a)-(c) shall indicate the date the materials were, or are intended to be, released to the security holders or soliciting individuals, as the case may be.

(e)

(1) **Public availability of information**. Preliminary copies filed pursuant to paragraph (a) shall be clearly marked as such. They shall be immediately available for public inspection unless ....

(2) **Confidential treatment for mergers etc**. ... action will be taken on any transaction specified in Item 14 of Schedule 14A, so long as:

(i) it is not a transaction subject to rule 13e–3 (going private) or Item 901(c) of Regulation S-K (roll-up);

(ii) the parties have not made any public communications relating to the transaction except for statements limited to the information specified in 1933 Act Rule 135; and

(iii) "The materials are filed in paper and marked 'Confidential, For Use of the Commission Only.'" In all cases, the materials may be disclosed to Congress and any US Government department or agency, and the Commission may make any necessary inquiries or investigation.

Instruction: If public communications go beyond the information specified in (iii), the materials must be re-filed promptly as public materials.

(f) "Communications not required to be filed. Copies of replies to inquiries from security holders requesting further information and copies of communications which do no more than request that forms of proxy theretofore solicited be signed and returned need not be filed pursuant to this section."

(g) **Notice of exempt solicitation under rule 14a-2(b)(1).**

  (1) "Any person who:

  (i) "Engages in a solicitation pursuant to rule 14a–2(b)(1), and

  (ii) At the commencement of that solicitation **owns** beneficially **securities** of the solicited class **with a market value of over $5 million**,

  shall mail to the Commission and any national securities exchange where any of the registrants securities are listed, within three days of first sending the solicitation or any additional communications to any security holder, a statement or amendment, as the case may be, containing the information specified in the Notice of Exempt Solicitation (§240.14a–103) and as an exhibit all written soliciting materials.

  (2) **However,** "no such submission need be made with respect to **oral solicitations** (other than with respect to scripts used in connection with such oral solicitations), speeches delivered in a public forum, press releases, published or broadcast opinions, statements, and **advertisements** appearing in a broadcast media, or a newspaper, magazine or other bona fide publication disseminated on a regular basis."

(h) Revised material. Any revised filing pursuant to this section shall indicate the revisions clearly and precisely, e.g. by means of underscoring.

(i) Fees. Filings are (2) free, except that (1) preliminary filings involving M&A transactions must include a non-refundable fee established in accordance with Rule 0–11.

(j) Merger proxy materials.

> (1) Materials need not be filed, and are deemed filed, under this section if they are (i) included in a registration statement filed under the 1933 Act on Forms S–4, F–4, or N–14; or (ii) filed under rules 424, 425, or 497 of the 1933 Act.

> (2) In this case, no fee needs to be paid under this section.

(k) "**Computing time periods**. In computing time periods beginning with the filing date specified in Regulation 14A (rules 14a–1 to 14b–1), the filing date shall be counted as the first day of the time period and midnight of the last day shall constitute the end of the specified time period."

(l) [Minimum 60-day notice period for roll-up transactions].

(m) "**Cover page**. Proxy materials filed with the Commission shall include a cover page in the form set forth in Schedule 14A. The cover page required by this paragraph need not be distributed to security holders."

(n) [Notice of exempt solicitation for roll-up transactions under rule 14a–2(b)(4)]

(o) Solicitations before furnishing a definitive proxy statement. … must be made in accordance with rule 14a–12 unless exempt under rule 14a–2.

14a-7   Obligations of registrants to provide a list of, or mail soliciting material to, security holders.

(a) If the registrant has made or intends to make a proxy solicitation, the **registrant must either provide a list** of security holders to, **or mail materials** for, any voting security holder[2] who so requests in writing. Upon receipt of such request, the registrant shall:

> (1) disclose to the requester within five business days:

---

[2] That is, any record or beneficial holder of securities entitled to vote at the meeting or consent in question.

(i) the registrant's election between mailing or providing the list;

(ii) "the approximate number of record holders and beneficial holders, separated by type of holder and class, ... which have been or are to be solicited on management's behalf, or any more limited group ... designated by the security holder if ... retrievable under the registrant's or its transfer agent's security holder data systems;" and

(iii) the estimated cost of mailing the materials to such holders;

(2) [either mail the materials for the soliciting holder or provide the list, the choice between the two being up to the registrant or the soliciting holder as specified in paragraph (b)]

(b) The **choice between mailing and list** belongs to

(1) the requesting security holder if the registrant's solicitation relates to a going private transaction under rule 13e-3 or [certain roll-up transactions];

(2) the registrant in all other cases.

(c) "At the time of a list request, the security holder making the request shall:"

(1) "If holding the registrant's securities through a nominee, provide the registrant with a statement by the nominee or other independent third party, or a copy of a current filing made with the Commission and furnished to the registrant, confirming such holder's beneficial ownership; and"

(2) Provide the registrant with an affidavit identifying the proposal or other corporate action that will be the subject of the security holder's solicitation and attesting that the security holder will comply with paragraph (d) below.

(d) "The security holder **shall not use the information** furnished by the registrant pursuant to paragraph (a)(2)(ii) for any purpose other than to solicit security holders with respect to the same meeting or action by consent ... for which the registrant is soliciting or intends to solicit ...; or disclose such information to any person other than an employee, agent, or beneficial owner for whom a request was made to the extent necessary to effectuate the communication or solicitation. The security holder shall return the information provided pursuant to paragraph (a)(2)(ii) … and shall not retain any copies thereof or of any information derived from such information after the termination of the solicitation."

(e) "The security holder **shall reimburse the reasonable expenses** incurred by the registrant in performing the acts requested pursuant to paragraph (a) of this section."

[Notes 1 and 2 to rule 14a–7 omitted]

14a-8   Shareholder proposals [OMITTED]

[The original is written in plain language, check it out on ecfr.gov etc.]

14a-9   False or misleading statements.

(a) No solicitation … shall … contain[] any statement which, at the time and in the light of the circumstances under which it is made, is <u>false or misleading with respect to any material fact</u>, **or which omits to state any material fact necessary in order to make the statements therein not false or misleading** or necessary to correct any statement in any earlier communication with respect to the solicitation of a proxy for the same meeting or subject matter which has become false or misleading."

(b) Examination of materials by the Commission does not entail a finding that such material is accurate or complete, or that the Commission has approved any statement contained therein.

(c) "No nominee, **nominating shareholder** or nominating shareholder group, or any member thereof, shall cause to be included in a registrant's proxy materials, … include in a notice on Schedule 14N, or include in any other related communication, any statement which, at the time and in the light of the circumstances under which it is made, is false or misleading with respect to any material fact …" (…: see para. (a)).

"Note: The following are some examples of what, depending upon particular facts and circumstances, may be misleading within the meaning of this section.

---

a. Predictions as to specific future market values.

b. Material which directly or indirectly impugns character, integrity or personal reputation, or directly or indirectly makes charges concerning improper, illegal or immoral conduct or associations, without factual foundation.

c. Failure to so identify a proxy statement, form of proxy and other soliciting material as to clearly distinguish it from the soliciting material of any other person or persons soliciting for the same meeting or subject matter.

d. Claims made prior to a meeting regarding the results of a solicitation."

14a-10   Prohibition of certain solicitations.

Nobody shall solicit any undated or postdated proxy.

[14a-11 et seq. OMITTED]

43261488R00057

Made in the USA
Middletown, DE
21 April 2019